RAISING
WISE
CHILDREN

HOW TO TEACH YOUR CHILD TO THINK

Carolyn
KOHLENBERGER

Noel
WESCOMBE

MULTNOMAH
Portland, Oregon 97266

Edited by Al Janssen and Rodney L. Morris
Cover design by Durand Demlow

RAISING WISE CHILDREN
© 1990 by Carolyn Kohlenberger and Noel Wescombe

Published by Multnomah Press
Portland, Oregon 97266

Multnomah Press is a ministry of Multnomah School of the Bible, 8435 Northeast Glisan Street, Portland, Oregon 97220.

Printed in the United States of America

Library of Congress Cataloging-in-Publication Data
Kohlenberger, Carolyn.
    Raising wise children : how to teach your child to think / Carolyn Kohlenberger, Noel Wescombe.
        p.   cm.
    Includes bibliographical references.
    ISBN 0-88070-326-1
    1. Cognition in children. 2. Child rearing—Religious aspects—Christianity. 3. Wisdom—Religious aspects—Christianity.
I. Wescombe, Noel. II. Title.
BF723.C5K62 1990
649'.68—dc20   89-29192
                                                          CIP

90 91 92 93 94 95 96 - 8 7 6 5 4 3 2 1

to

Sarah Kohlenberger
Joshua Kohlenberger
and
Meghan Wescombe

Contents

Acknowledgments

Writing a book, like wise thinking, is often best accomplished with help from other people. I would like to thank the following friends and family for their contributions throughout the many stages of this project:

Kin Millen said, "That's a good idea," then proved he meant it.

Rollie Aden helped with writing at the very beginning.

Gene Takalo passed on articles and ideas.

The tutors and teacher's assistants at Good Shepherd School helped with fine-tuning our survey.

Al Janssen and Rod Morris gave practical and much appreciated editorial assistance.

Dr. Randall Nelson graciously provided relevant journal articles and professional advice concerning the project in general, and the survey specifically.

Becky Dickman, Linda Hill, Kathy Jirak, and Doris Kohlenberger held my hand and my heart.

Cathie Wescombe proofread, commented on early manuscript drafts, and faithfully supported Noel as he worked on the book.

My husband, John, often rearranged his work schedule to accommodate mine, tirelessly answered hundreds of computer questions, and provided needed encouragement to his sometimes frazzled wife.

Special thanks to my parents, Jack and Betty Nelson, who first taught me to think, and continue to do so today.

Who Teaches Your Child to Think?

The old farmhouse was battered by the wind. Sucked up into the eye of the tornado, it tossed and spun. Gradually the gale subsided, and the house dropped from the sky, landing with a jarring crash.

Dorothy emerged from a crooked doorway. In her arms she held a little dog. Together they surveyed the broken house and the land on which it now rested. "Toto," she said, "I have a feeling we're not in Kansas anymore."

Those of us who grew up in the fifties and early sixties could make similar remarks about the world we live in today. We didn't go anywhere, but our society is not the one we remember. We have to navigate through new, uncertain surroundings. And we must guide our children as well.

We need to take a look at our children's world and the choices they must make. The problems of their generation are light-years removed from our own childhood dilemmas. During those years we got by quite well with a few simple directions (cross with the light, don't take candy from strangers, don't smoke, don't swear, and be kind to animals). But the complex problems kids face today cannot be solved by simple rules and simple thinking. Times have changed. Lifestyles have changed. And the future has changed for all of us.

The New, Revised America

America is still reeling from a cultural explosion that shook our country to its foundation. Its fallout showered our lives with choices. Every day we hear about a new idea, a new product, a new job, or a new moral code.

Most Americans enjoy their new choice-filled lifestyle. In fact, some have embraced it so fully that they change their job, religion, and moral standards more often than they change the oil in their car. Many of these new choices make us feel blessed. But just as many make us wary, fearful, and downright scared. If we're not careful, we can easily get ulcers from our new choice-rich diet. Making wise decisions has become a job for experts, and we must be the experts to survive.

Two aspects of life have undergone the most change. First, traditional moral standards were questioned, then discarded by many in the late sixties and early seventies. Most of us know all about that. But second, in the last twenty years fewer new jobs were created in industry and farming. Now information is our biggest business. In fact, over half of work done today centers around facts, ideas, and communication.[1] Making sense out of data has become a matter of daily routine. But just as moral choices require more thought today, working with information demands more thinking and decision making than most of us have been trained to do.

New ideas are popping up all over. New ways of using those ideas are developed daily. Morals shift and bend with the wind. Sometimes we're so overburdened with choices, we don't know which way to turn. Yet if we are confused, how must our kids feel? This is the only way of life they have ever known. They have no roots in a more stable past. How can we prepare them for this world of information, choice, and lax morality?

The Critical Thinking Movement

Parents are not alone in the struggle. Educators have worked hard to find a solution to this problem. For years they watched as students floundered in the ocean of moral choices, new concepts, and vast quantities of information. Students were memorizing facts, but they were often unable to use the facts they had learned. They faced a future of choices and decisions in which their memorization skills would be of little help. Clearly a new approach was needed.

Sink or swim?—that was the question. The educational experts decided the answer was mental swimming lessons. If kids could be trained to think well and learn to make good choices, they would be prepared to survive on their own in the sea of new ideas and data. Courses on thinking were developed. Concepts taught in those classes were later applied to other subjects as well. Students began learning thinking skills in their English, mathematics, and science courses.

Teaching thinking has gained wide acceptance. Today, students all over the world receive thinking training from kindergarten through college. In fact, the U.S. has been slower than many nations to jump on the bandwagon. But we are quickly catching up. By 1985 public schools in over half of the states offered this training.[2] Many private and Christian schools have followed suit, teaching the concept they call "critical thinking."

But what is "critical thinking"? Robert Ennis, an expert in thinking skills, defines it this way: "Critical thinking is reflective and reasonable thinking that is focused on deciding what to believe or do."[3] Instead of simply memorizing facts, critical thinking works toward the goal of better understanding. It often leads to a decision about how to act or what to believe.

Students are learning many new ways to think. They are taught to analyze ideas and material, to brainstorm, to predict future outcomes, to find creative answers, to identify propaganda, and to problem-solve. Using these methods, students are able to make more careful decisions. And critical thinking prepares students to be independent learners. It's no wonder educators see this new emphasis on thinking as a hope for the future.

Surprisingly, as new and revolutionary as these thinking methods may sound, most are not new at all. Over two thousand years ago, Socrates taught these kinds of skills.[4] You and I know many adults who didn't receive critical thinking training in school, yet think critically every day. These skills can be acquired by trial and error, but it takes time and practice.

Unfortunately, kids today don't have the luxury of waiting around. Broadening moral and career choices in our society makes thinking skills a necessary tool for survival. They are a vital preparation for deciding what to believe and do in the present and in the future. But we must ask the question, Are schools the best and only place for our children to learn to think and make decisions? Are schools the only place where we want our children to decide what they believe and how they should act?

Learning Thinking Skills in the Classroom

Most Americans assume that schools are the best place for children to learn. And it seems a logical assumption that along with the ABCs, kids would be taught to be good thinkers. But are schools the best place for children to learn to think? For several reasons, the answer is no.

It is difficult to practice thinking skills in school. One of the most important keys to becoming a wise thinker is practice, practice, and more practice. Learning to think is like learning to ride a bike. At first you make lots of mistakes. Then with each attempt, you learn something new. If you practice enough, eventually you begin to look like a pro.

Thinking is a skill that improves with practice. But in order to be most helpful, new skills must be applied to real-life or close to real-life experiences. Regretfully, many teachers are unable, and sometimes not willing, to provide the hours, one-to-one attention, and realistic situations such intense practice requires. As a result, many students never use the skills taught in class.[5]

Imagine trying to learn to ride a bike by reading instructions in a textbook. Until you have a chance to test your knowledge on the street with your bike, the directions won't be much good. And even after reading the book, chances are you still couldn't jump on the saddle and ride off into the sunset any better than your friend who skipped class the day you covered bike riding. Students who learn about thinking skills in the classroom are in much the same predicament. They come away from class with tips on how to improve their thinking, but without frequent use and practical application, new skills will never become life-long habits.

Children learn to think at different rates and in different ways. Anyone of normal intelligence can improve their thinking.[6] But each of us has areas of strength and weakness. We also learn at different rates. A skill your child will pick up in a day may take weeks or months for my child to learn.

When my daughter, Sarah, was an infant, I remember how concerned I was about her learning to walk. A friend of mine had a daughter the same age, and her little girl began running around by her ninth month. But Sarah took her time and, like an average child, did not walk until she was a year old. During those few months in between, I remember thinking, "Will she ever learn? Why is she slower?" Yet as anyone who knows her can attest, Sarah now runs with the best of them. She learned to walk when it was her time to walk.

Learning thinking in a classroom may involve pressure and fear of failure. Learning in class is often pressure-filled. Those who pick up a skill more slowly feel pressed to catch up with the rest. Kids who fall behind are often labeled as failures by peers and teachers. What could be worse than feeling like a failure at thinking? A youngster who is labeled "dummy" by others all too often sees himself in that role for the rest of his life. What a waste to the world and to the cause of Christ! Wise thinking is too important to entrust totally to others. Parents must be sure their kids have plenty of thinking practice at home *and* at school.

Thinking teachers teach values and beliefs that often do not match the values and beliefs of the parents. Lack of practice, too little time, and peer pressure are disadvantages of teaching thinking in schools. But another problem is even more serious. Critical thinking trains kids to analyze, evaluate, and make judgments. Every step of this process depends on values and beliefs. Depending on what we value, a logical decision may not be a wise choice. A teenager might think, "I need to get to school on time. If I drive faster I will not be tardy. No police car is around so I can run this stop sign." Her thinking is technically correct. Going faster and running stop signs will probably help her arrive at school more quickly. But while getting to school on time is good, other greater values are missing. She does not have high regard for the law or the safety of herself and others. As a result, she may end up causing an accident and may never get to school again. Values play a major role in the choices we make. We must ask, "What kind of values are my children picking up as they learn to think critically?"

Values are being taught in schools, but not in a consistent way. Some educators have suggested that schools should adopt a common social morality as a guideline.[7] Students would then learn to make decisions based on this moral code. This approach may be better than teachers having free reign, but for the moral code to be acceptable to a cross-section of parents, it will not be based on the standards Christians embrace. Few Bible-believing parents will find this compromise totally acceptable.

Until such a moral code is adopted, teachers choose what values are taught. Some teach their personal beliefs. Others leave moral judgments up to the student. But how many school-aged children have fully developed values? Without help, how many children can apply their own beliefs to a decision? And how many teachers "offer help" that persuades students to question or abandon their Christian views? Will students learn there is one way to think at school and another way to think at home? That is very possible. Schools are teaching thinking, but they are also teaching values. Parents must ask, "Are the values being taught *my* values?"

One of the greatest desires of Christian parents is for their children to behave in a Christ-like manner. But children who do not know how to think using biblical values cannot make wise choices. We cannot hope they will act better than they think. The values they learn in thinking training in school (and this includes Christian schools as well as public) are often not the only values Christian parents would like them to consider in their choices and decisions.

Schools will continue to teach critical thinking, so parents must teach their children at home that there is more to thinking than those skills taught in class. God has given us minds to use for his glory. We must help our children learn to combine good thinking with God's values. In this age of choice, lax morals, and over-abundance of information, parents must take the initiative to teach their children how to think with wisdom.

Raising Wise Children will show you how you can teach your child to be a Wisdom Thinker. By that I don't mean your five-year-old will begin to make decisions like a Supreme Court judge. But I do mean that given thinking skill training, your child will have the tools he needs for making better choices. He will be able to make the most of his ability to think. As years go by, his skill in using those tools will increase. By the time he reaches adulthood, he'll be able to put Wisdom Thinking to good use.

The first section of this book is all about Wisdom Thinking. We'll explain what it is and how to do it well. The second section is about children. You'll find out how they learn and how to teach them thinking skills. The third section is a collection of thinking games and activities. You can pick and choose from these methods to teach wise thinking to your child, whether preschooler or teenager.

Raising Wise Children is not about molding your child into an eggheaded genius. Noel and I aren't going to give any tips on passing SATs or getting into the best colleges. This is a book about Wisdom Thinking. Life-changing thinking. The kind of thinking our Christian children need to use to survive in our world of choice and change.

Introduction, Notes

1. Harlan Cleveland, "Educating Citizens and Leaders for an Information-Based Society," *The Education Digest*, September 1986.

2. "Why Johnny Can't Reason," *Newsweek*, 27 January 1986, 59.

3. Robert H. Ennis, "A Logical Basis for Measuring Critical Thinking Skills," *Educational Leadership*, October 1985, 45.

4. Richard W. Paul, "The Critical Thinking Movement," *Phi Kappa Phi Journal* (Winter 1985):2.

5. Michael Scriven, "Critical for Survival," *Phi Kappa Phi Journal* (Winter 1985):9.

6. "Clear Thinking May Depend On the 'Hat' You Wear, An Interview With Edward de Bono," *U.S. News & World Report*, 2 December 1985, 75.

7. Gary Bauer, "Teaching Morality in the Classroom," *The Education Digest*, March 1987, 2-5.

Section One

Understanding
Wisdom Thinking

CHAPTER ONE

Beginnings
of Wisdom

The serpent fascinated Eve. Long and green, dew sparkling on his scales, he was unlike any serpent she had met in the Garden. The others were nice to watch. But this serpent seemed different from the rest. Truly in a class by himself.

"Did God really say, 'You must not eat from any tree in the garden'?" the serpent asked Eve.

She replied, "We may eat fruit from the trees in the garden, but God did say, 'You must not eat fruit from the tree that is in the middle of the garden, and you must not touch it, or you will die.' "

Eve was quite sure this was the right answer. She even added the part about not touching the fruit to impress the serpent with how much she knew. But he wasn't impressed. In fact, he had some news for her.

The serpent said, "You will not surely die. For God knows that when you eat of it your eyes will be opened, and you will be like God, knowing good and evil."

The fruit, which Eve had never before considered eating, suddenly looked enticing. One bite would give her the chance to know things that only God knew, things he was keeping from her and Adam.

The choice was simple. Without further thought, Eve reached up, plucked the fruit from the tree, and ate. Then she gave some to Adam, and he ate too.

At that moment the need for Wisdom Thinking was born.

When God asked Eve why she had eaten the fruit, she said, "The serpent deceived me, and I ate." It was her only defense.

If Eve's future rested in the hands of a judge in an American court today, she would certainly get off with a light sentence. After all, she was naive. The poor woman had fallen into a bad crowd. And she had no record of previous offenses.

But God didn't save Eve from the consequences of her actions. Instead he handed down the maximum penalty because he knew Eve had been prepared to make a wise decision. She had been given the knowledge to do what was right. The choice was hers. And she chose to eat the fruit.

Each day our children must make choices too. And like Eve, they must face the consequences of their choices. Often consequences are not small.

Look what happened to these kids:

- After ruining her brother's radio, Tina blamed the damage on her sister, Rene. Rene was punished; Tina got away scot-free . . . except that Rene refused to forget.

- Michael was not to trade toys with friends without his parents' permission. But he did it anyway. When a "new toy" appeared at home, he explained that he was just borrowing it for the day. But his sister spilled the beans. His parents grounded him for a double-length of time for lying as well as disobeying.

- Ben watched while his friends vandalized a neighbor's house. The police arrived and Ben was taken to the police station along with the rest.

- Dana's boyfriend asked for a more physical relationship. Fearing he'd drop her if she said no, she consented, and became pregnant. Then he dropped her.

We must prepare our children for choices like these. Though some may seem simple to make, others may take years to resolve. But all require careful, wise thinking. For even the simplest choice can be a trap arranged by a serpent-in-waiting. Just ask Eve.

A WORD FROM THE WISE

Wisdom is supreme; therefore get wisdom.
Though it cost all you have, get understanding.

(Proverbs 4:7)

Solomon's wise sayings recorded in the Book of Proverbs have guided generations throughout the centuries. This exalted king of Israel knew the value of wisdom. By the time he uttered his first proverbs, Solomon had been around the palace a few times. He had learned the cost of foolishness by making some king-sized boo-boos. And, though he continued to make many poor choices throughout the rest of his life, his wealth of experience gave him a vast store of earthly wisdom.

In addition to his experience, "God gave Solomon wisdom and very great insight, and a breadth of understanding as measureless as the sand on the seashore" (1 Kings 4:29). Kings sent envoys to learn wise thinking at his feet (1 Kings 4:34). We should sit at his feet too. We need to learn from wise thinkers throughout history, and from wise thinkers alive today. Tina, Nate, Ben, and Dana need their wise advice. Our children need it too.

The Skills of a Wise Thinker

What *do* wise thinkers have in common? How do they think? What do they know? What can we learn from them that we can teach to our children so they can be wise thinkers too?

Noel and I asked these questions throughout our research. Our reading took us from biblical records to modern accounts. As we read, three basic skills wise thinkers have in common kept popping up over and over again. We saw these three skills in the Old and New Testaments. The labels were different, but we met them again in the methods of Socrates and in modern papers on "critical thinking."

Old ideas, new names. And we determined that all three skills are essential to wise thinking. Seeing how they worked together, we formed the concept of Wisdom Thinking.

Whatever your child's age, you can begin to teach him to be a Wisdom Thinker. But if this seems like unfamiliar territory for you, join the crowd! Teaching children to think is not something most moms and dads have been trained to do. None of my Family Life and Parenting classes in college even touched on teaching thinking. And when Noel and I asked over a hundred parents in a survey about how they are raising their children, we found few parents felt they fully understood how to teach their child to think. So if you're feeling a little out of your league, you're not alone.

Even if this is your first attempt at teaching thinking skills, you'll catch on to the concepts quickly. The three skills won't be hard for you to understand. They aren't strange or unusual. In fact, you'll find you already use some of these skills each day as you make your own choices. We'll help you put them together in an organized way so that you can effectively teach them to your child. So let's get started by previewing the three skills of Wisdom Thinking.

THE THREE SKILLS OF WISDOM THINKING

Skill One—Gathering, Sorting, and Choosing

The first skill of Wisdom Thinking is a three-step process. The first step is *gathering* information. The second step is *sorting* what has been gathered.

The third step is *choosing* what to believe or do. Together they form the first of the three essential skills of Wisdom Thinking.

We *gather* information almost constantly. We hear or read a new fact or idea, and we store it away. We see a new object and we remember it. We touch, smell, and taste what is around us, and we tuck the memory away. As we grow, the amount of information we've stored inside our head grows too. But sometimes our old "inside" information isn't enough to be helpful for deciding what to believe or do. More data is needed from the "outside." Then we go out and gather new "outside" information and add it to the old "inside" information. Used together, we have enough information to do some wise thinking.

As a school librarian, I have many opportunities to help students gather facts and ideas for assignments. Sandi came to me one day asking for help on a report. To get the gathering process started, I first asked her what she already knew about her subject. Then we used that inside information to gather as much new outside information as we could find. Her new findings, combined with her previous knowledge, gave her a greater understanding of her subject.

But gathering information is not enough when deciding what to believe or do. Thinkers must learn to *sort* what is useful from what is not. Information that is not helpful must be identified and tossed out. And we must be able to identify facts and ideas that can help us make a wise decision.

After Sandi gathered, she sorted through what she had collected. She had to decide what was useful to complete her assignment. Some information was interesting but did not help her on this particular paper. Other information was unusable because it was out of date. This she discarded too. When sorting was done, she had some good solid facts to use when completing her assignment.

Gathering and sorting are the beginning steps that help us make choices. When we have sorted and found what options are open to us, we must then *choose* what we will believe or do.

Choosing for Sandi was deciding what she would believe, which facts she would use, and how she would use them. Her finished report was a result of gathering, sorting, and choosing.

Gathering, sorting, and choosing is an organized plan of action children and adults can learn. It can make their thinking more careful and wise.

To picture this in another way, imagine you own a factory where you make apple pies. Inside the factory you have the equipment to do the work, the spices and sugar, even the pie crust. But you have no apples, and apples are an essential ingredient for making apple pies. You need help from outside.

So you go outside to the orchard and *gather* as many apples as you can. If you gather many bushels, your chance of getting some good apples is better. And if you pick different kinds of apples (Newton, Granny Smith, Rome Beauty), you will be more likely to find a combination that will make your pie taste unique, and reflect God's creativity.

You take the apples to your factory and dump them on the conveyor belt. As it rolls by, you *sort* them. Some cannot be used because they're rotten or bruised, but others are just right. The best are sent on to be cut up, mixed with your spices and sugar, and poured into crusts. Then you bake all the ingredients together. Out of those finished pies, tasting reveals the best pie. You *choose* that pie to serve to your customers.

If you did a good job gathering, sorting, and choosing, you probably ended up with a pretty tasty pie. But mistakes can bring ruin to even the best factories. Gathering can be haphazard and incomplete. You could work too quickly and fail to sort out all the bad apples from the good. Or you might over- or under-bake the pies.

Fortunately, these and other problems can be avoided (chapter 2 will explain how). With careful gathering, sorting, and choosing, the quality of the end product will be just what you need.

Children who learn gathering, sorting, and choosing generally do better in their school work and personal thinking than children who have not learned this skill. You can teach gathering, sorting, and choosing to your child, young or old. But it is only the first of the three skills of Wisdom Thinking. There are two more skills that must be added to make good thinking even better.

Skill Two—Thinking about Thinking

The second skill of Wisdom Thinking is *thinking about thinking*. This skill has three parts as well. The first part is looking ahead—it is planning how to think. The second part is keeping a close eye on thinking while gathering, sorting, and choosing. The third part is looking back to see how well thinking was done.

Many children learn to think about thinking in school. If your child has taken courses in *critical thinking,* she's learned some of these skills already. Or she might have learned them as part of English, science, or math. Find out if your child is learning critical thinking at school. It can make a big difference in the way she is able to solve problems or work with ideas.

My son, Josh, took his first critical thinking course in second grade. It helped him think about thinking when his feelings were hurt one day at school. On our way home, Josh told me a classmate had made fun of his yellow and black soccer ball. This classmate told everyone it was "dumb" because real soccer balls were *white* and black. He said any other color wasn't official.

I asked Josh what he thought about that. He replied, "I like my soccer ball. Uncle Randy gave it to me. And besides, what he said isn't a *fact,* it's just his *opinion.*" I wanted to know where Josh had learned to tell the difference between facts and opinions. "In critical thinking," he replied. "Lesson three."

Because of his critical thinking class, Josh, at age seven, was able to analyze the way his friend had been thinking. It helped him weigh the value of his friend's words.

Now go back to your apple pie factory. Thinking about Thinking (TAT) takes the role of your plant manager. She checks to see that all the machinery is in working order before the conveyor belt begins to roll. TAT makes sure all the workers are in their stations. Then she carefully watches them while they work. She listens to the machines. Knowing one wrench in the gears could throw the factory off line, she makes sure that never happens. None of the workers take naps when she's around. Under her careful eye, machines are well maintained and run smoothly. TAT is always observing, pointing out problems, correcting. When the workday is through, she fills out her report. She tells what went well, and what didn't. The next day, adjustments will be made based on what TAT says.

Thinking about thinking protects the outcome of your thought process. Knowing where problems can pop up, and seeing to it that they don't, keeps thinking on track. Just being aware of thinking traps and common errors can help most thinkers improve their choice making. But one last skill is needed to make good thinking into Wisdom Thinking.

Skill Three—Thinking about God

Thinking about God is the third skill of Wisdom Thinking. Again, it has three parts. The first part is learning to use God's Word as part of thinking, the second part is listening to wise counselors, and the third part is praying while thinking. Without the skill of Thinking about God, we are no better than human computers. A computer can give a logical answer, but logical answers are not always the best answers. Elements of loving, caring, and eternal perspective cannot be programmed into computers. But they are part of people. And they are part of God's plan for his people.

Commands and examples in the Bible set the standard for what we should believe and do. Where there are no clear directions, we have been given principles which guide our thinking and choices. And just as TAT keeps the machinery working, Thinking about God (TAG) insures cleanliness, purity, and a more perfect wisdom.

Back to the pie factory one last time. TAG oversees the work with TAT, though TAG has more seniority. In his hands he holds the "Recipe" for the best apple pie the world has ever tasted. The workers look to him for direction. When he says something isn't right, no one sleeps until the problem is corrected. He roams the factory, checking to see that workers are working for the right reason. He knows cleanliness must be up to standard. Since his knowledge of apples is unsurpassed, he is best able to look for disease and flaws that would make the apple pies impure. When the new apples are being mixed with the old, he sees that they are in the proper proportion. And when the pies are done, he tastes them to see if they measure up to the Recipe he knows is best. His is the final check before the pies leave the factory.

Thinking about God and his standards makes thinking wise. Our recipe is his Word. Following that recipe will help us believe and do what is right. God gives direction to our thoughts. We can measure new ideas by his standards and principles. When we add new ideas and facts to our bank of knowledge, the balance must be in favor of his ideas over ours. And when we complete the thinking process by making choices, his standard must be our final authority.

If your child begins at an early age believing God has a place in her thinking process, she will be miles ahead of her peers who may learn it later in life or perhaps not at all. She *can* do the right things for the right reasons. Being aware of how God wants her to think and act adds a whole new perspective to choosing what to believe and do. That perspective is what makes thinking wise.

You have been introduced to the three skills of Wisdom Thinking. We've gone over them quickly just to give you an idea of what wise thinkers do when they think. Now it's time to stop and catch your breath. You probably have tons of questions about the skills, and maybe you have some doubts about how well you can learn them. That's natural. But don't worry—Noel and I don't expect you to understand them completely right this minute. We're going to slow down and look at each skill carefully. Your questions will be answered.

Before you read on, fill out the section below. You say you don't ever do the suggested activities in books? Often I don't either. But, I promise, there are no trick questions, and it will only take a couple of minutes. It's important that you do it because you will learn more about the skills we've just talked about by actually doing some step-by-step thinking. So relax. Mark up your book—nobody's looking! (Not even this librarian!)

YOU TRY IT!

You've just read about Wisdom Thinking. Now let's practice. On the lists below, pick an idea you would like to investigate and pick a problem you want to solve. Circle one of our suggestions or write in your own idea or problem at the bottom of each list. You'll be using your chosen idea and problem to practice Wisdom Thinking at the end of the next three chapters.

Ideas

- friendship
- discipleship
- abortion
- civil disobedience
- debt
- wealth
- love
- _____

Problems

- What car should I buy?
- What house should I buy?
- What type of schooling should my son or daughter receive?
- My parents are getting old. How can I help them best?
- Should I use credit cards?
- _____

Things for your young Wisdom Thinker to do

Now involve your child:

- Ask your child to tell you something she wants to buy.
- Ask your child to tell you something he wants to do.
- I want to buy:
- _____
- I want to do:
- _____

That's it! Now let's learn more about gathering, sorting, and choosing.

CHAPTER TWO

Skill One:
Gathering, Sorting,
and Choosing

A stranger walked to the front of the synagogue. Tired, worn, and squinty-eyed, he had the look of a man who didn't know where he would find his next meal. He said his name was Paul, and he had come to Berea to tell about Jesus, the Christ, who had died and had risen from the dead.

If Paul looked a little nervous, he had good reason. He had been run out of Thessalonica just a few days before after preaching the same message he was about to preach today. Now he looked at the faces upturned before him. Were they angry? Offended? No, they seemed calm and interested.

Paul spoke that day and for several more days

in a row. The scene was always the same. When the sermon time came, the Bereans were eager to *gather* in what he had to say. But they didn't just listen. They "examined the Scriptures . . . to see if what Paul said was true" (Acts 17:11). Though Paul was persuasive, the Bereans *sorted* through his claims and made sure they matched up with the rest of Scripture.

When the Bereans were convinced that Paul was speaking the truth, they made their *choice*. "Many of the Jews believed, as did also a number of prominent Greek women and many Greek men" (v.12).

These listeners with ears to hear will forever be remembered as Luke describes them: The noble Bereans. But they gained much more than high honor. Careful gathering, sorting, and choosing led them to the truth. It led them to a life of fellowship with God.

Gathering, sorting, and choosing is the foundation for wise choice making. You can begin teaching these three steps to your child after you finish reading the next few pages. But remember, learning to think is a step-by-step process. It takes time and practice. Be patient, and look forward to the day when your child thinks like a Berean.

TAKING THE FIRST STEP: GATHERING INFORMATION

The heart of the discerning acquires
    knowledge;
the ears of the wise seek it out.

Proverbs 18:15

The goal of gathering is to find as many facts and ideas as possible about a problem to be solved or an idea to be investigated.

Do you like to shop? I do. Because most facts and ideas don't carry a price tag, gathering is like shopping when all clothes are free. Imagine you need some new clothes for your high school reunion. If you could gather clothes like you can gather facts and ideas, you would walk through a department store and take home any outfits you think *might* be okay. If you really got into gathering, you would drive home with an overflowing U-Haul trailing behind you. Because you gathered so many different styles and colors, chances are that somewhere in your mile-high pile is a wonderful dress or suit. At the very least, you'll have several that will be terrific. This is the whole point of gathering. It opens up options. It provides many different ways to solve problems and investigate ideas.

Gathering as much information as possible is important for all of us to learn. When I don't gather carefully when my children have a fight, I make bad judgments about who was right and who was wrong. I need to constantly remind myself to make sure I have the whole story before I think any further. Most kids have tunnel vision when it comes to problem solving. Unless they've been taught to search for new information and solutions, they usually think of only one way to solve a problem.

Wendy desperately wanted the "in" hair barrettes all the girls in her class were wearing. But at five dollars each, her parents said no. Whenever Wendy went to the store, she was tempted to steal one. Fortunately, before she acted on her impulse, she shared her anguish with her grandmother. Grandma went to the store with Wendy, looked at the barrettes, and took Wendy home. Using some of

Wendy's plain hair clips, some ribbon, glue, and beads, she created original designs that Wendy loved.

Most problems have several possible solutions. Wendy's grandmother helped her see that she had other choices besides buying or stealing.

Inside and Outside Information

There are two places where your child should learn to gather facts and ideas: inside her head and outside her head.

Returning to our apple pie illustration, inside the factory are the ingredients the company already owns. Sugar, spices, and pie dough. If the company wants to make pastry, these ingredients might be enough to do the job.

Sometimes your child can solve problems just by using "inside" information, those facts and ideas she has been gathering since birth. Show her how to make use of her inside information.

Six-year-old Mitch bullied his younger brother. To help him see why he should stop, his mother asked him to imagine how his brother felt. Remembering when he was bullied by another boy in the neighborhood, Mitch recalled how helpless he felt and how much he disliked the boy who tormented him. Even at six, he had memories to gather and use.

Allison wanted to go on a date, but her parents did not approve of the boy who asked her out. She considered lying to them and going anyway. Her older sister suggested to Allison that she think of all the reasons why she should go, and the reasons why she shouldn't. Allison then listed all the possible results of both options. She decided not to go. Her new problem was solved with old information.

"Outside" the brain is new information which can be gathered from many sources. When children are young, most outside info comes from parents, brothers, and sisters. Later, friends and teachers become new places to go gathering. In time, libraries and experts become valued gathering sources.

Back at the factory, outside information is found in the orchard. Apples are new facts and ideas. When added to what's already in the factory, they made delicious apple pies.

When kids have dilemmas, they often go to parents as their orchard of information. You can take these opportunities to show your child how to decide what to do. And you can use these moments to teach her how to gather information. Be her number one source. You can give out facts and ideas she would never think to consider. Spur her on to Wisdom Thinking.

Take your child to the library and look up information together. If you don't know how to use any resource books, ask. Librarians are there to help you. They'll not only show you where to find a book, they'll help you learn how to use it. Use the yellow pages to locate government information sources. Call and ask your question. Take advantage of the free brochures they offer. Read newspapers, books, and magazines in your home. Parents who rarely read books raise children who rarely read. Uninformed moms and dads raise children who are unaware of world events. Take the lead and show your child how to gather from outside sources. Whatever the problem, she should never lack for facts and ideas. We live in a nation that thrives on information. It's there for the taking. Take some.

What to Take, What to Leave

When gathering information, the rule is: Take whatever seems to apply to the problem. The more gathered, the better. But some facts and ideas should be left behind. Some don't help solve the problem. Facts from less-than-reliable sources should be gathered with reservation. Gather only what helps you make your choice and only what helps you think about your idea.

THE SECOND STEP: SORTING

Sorting is picking through and arranging what has been gathered. The goal is to see what will help and what will not. Sorting narrows down options. It shows possible solutions to a problem, or gives better understanding of an idea.

In the apple pie factory, the apples go down the conveyor belt to be picked over by the workers. Those that are obviously rotten are discarded. Those that are underripe are tossed. Any that have worms peeking out are gingerly shoved aside.

The apples are then separated according to type. The Newtons go to one conveyor belt, Rome Beauties another. The Golden Delicious roll off on their own. Each type makes a pie, but each tastes a little different than the others. Depending on what the customer wants, one type of pie will be the preferred solution to his problem.

Wise thinking requires sorting to separate and categorize facts and ideas. Sorting can be done chronologically—which fact came first? Facts can also be arranged by source—who said what? They can also be arranged by type—which facts and ideas work together? Then you can sort by priority—most important to least important; best to worst. After looking closely, some facts and ideas cannot be used. Some are not closely related to the problem, others are unworkable.

Andy wanted to buy a new bike. After saving his money for several months, he was still fifty dollars short. He wrote down his own solution ideas and then asked friends for help. Here is his list of options: Borrow money from Mom and Dad. Ask for money for birthday. Mow lawns. Baby-sit. Rob a bank. Look for the bike on sale. Ask Mom and Dad to give me money out of college fund. Write a letter to bike company complaining that their prices are too high.

When Andy asked his parents for money from them or his college fund, they refused. Writing the company was probably a lost cause. This solution did not relate closely enough to his problem. Robbing a bank was criminal, thus unworkable. But asking for birthday money, mowing lawns, baby-sitting, and looking for sales were all good possibilities.

Next Andy grouped similar ideas together. One group was his "working options" (lawn mowing, baby-sitting). The other group was his "wishful thinking options" (birthday money, sales). Looking at the two types of options, he decided that the wishful thinking options weren't a dependable source of money. He decided his chances of getting the needed money would be better by choosing an option in the working group.

Sorting Reveals Options

Sorting reveals options. It narrows down possibilities. But it also shows paths that are good possible solutions. These should be further examined. Teach your child to think each path through to a conclusion. Help him test those that might work. One might be better than the others, but it is hard to know unless they are all investigated to the end.

One of the best illustrations of this idea comes from a modern thinking-teacher named Edward de Bono. It features a man who needs to find water. He decides to dig a well. After digging many feet down, he finds no moisture. Determined to find water, he digs deeper. But his problem isn't the depth of his well. His problem is that he has dug in the wrong place. If he keeps on digging, he may learn a lot about backaches and hard labor, but if he doesn't find water, he hasn't solved his problem. But if he abandons the first hole and digs other holes ten or twenty feet away, he could find an underground spring just below the surface.

Sometimes it is necessary to follow a solution to the end only to find it must be left behind. Sorting can help reveal which options might work. Looking at each option in turn can help determine which is the most likely to be a wise choice.

THE GIANT STEP: CHOOSING

The goal of choosing is to make the best possible choice about what to believe or do. It changes or reaffirms thinking or actions.

At PIE Inc., the goal of every effort is to produce good apple pies. After apples are gathered, sorted, and mixed with the spices and sugar, they are baked. If the oven temperature is too hot or the pies are baked too long, the pies burn. If the oven temperature is too cold or the pies are baked too quickly, they turn out doughy and undercooked. Neither will please the customer. But if the conditions and ingredients are good, the pies are just right.

Half-baked Thinking

Half-baked ideas and solutions are the result of too little thinking.

> It is not good to have zeal without
> knowledge,
> nor to be hasty and miss the way.
>
> Proverbs 19:2

For weeks Melissa had planned to have her birthday party at an expensive amusement park. A few days before the big event, her mother told her she could only invite two friends. Thinking quickly, Melissa selected two friends from school, forgetting her oldest and best friend who had just moved to the other side of town. Melissa had previously invited her. So at the appointed time, her friend arrived for the party, sending Melissa and her mother into an embarrassed silence. Good thinking isn't always quick thinking.

Over-baking

Over-baking is refusing to make a choice. The end of thinking is some sort of decision. Hannah put off choosing a college because her favorite didn't accept her, and she couldn't face being away from her friends. Theo put off choosing his college because the three he had to choose from seemed so similar. He wanted someone else to choose what was best for him.

Help your child learn to choose. Be a partner in thinking all the way through the process. Be sure your child knows all her options and understands them. Explain which seem the best and why, but don't choose for her unless she absolutely will not make a choice. If a decision can be held off without irreparable damage, let your child experience the consequences of not choosing.

Choosing Not to Choose

Choosing not to choose is different from not choosing. After completely thinking a problem or idea through, your child may find no workable solution. If this happens when a decision isn't required immediately, her thinking can be done over again. Perhaps gathering was not thorough. Or sorting was sloppy. Or perhaps she learned enough to know there was even more she should learn before choosing.

Choosing not to choose is not bad. It can allow for more "baking time," which can make a choice clearer. This extra time can let your child become comfortable with the options before her. Choosing not to choose can be a sign of a careful, perceptive thinker.

Taking the Plunge

When I go toy shopping with my children, the moments I dread are when they must choose between similar items that cost the same amount.

They can't choose by color, shape, design, or price. Taking the plunge is the only option left. They won't know if it's a good choice until the wrapper comes off and they use it for a while.

Your child will have to take the choice plunge sometimes. When a choice must be made, but no option seems best, teach her to try one and see how it goes. If it doesn't work, very likely she can try again. At the very least, she may learn not to use that choice next time.

Is This the End?

Choosing is *sort of* the end of the thinking process, but it isn't really the end. After a choice has been made, you must teach your child to ask, "How did I do? Did I solve my problem? Did I find out what I wanted to know? Is this solution working well? Should I abandon this solution and try another of my options?"

The goal of Wisdom Thinking is to make wise choices. It's a worthy goal to want to think like a Berean. Their willingness to gather new information, sort through it, and make a choice led them to the place where God wanted them to be. You can teach your child to make choices like a Berean too.

Remember the thinking you did at the end of chapter 1? Now that you've read more about gathering, sorting, and choosing, it's time to try out what you've learned.

YOU TRY IT!

Things for you to do with your young Wisdom Thinker

If you're like most people, you have a "junk" drawer in your kitchen. I keep our flashlight and some batteries in our junk drawer. There are some coupons and scissors in it too. No telling what's hiding below the paper in the back. Find a drawer something like my junk drawer at your house and dump it out on the table. Better yet, have your child find it and then dump it out on the table.

Gather

Have your child gather the items together in a neater arrangement. But don't do any sorting yet. Use the word *gather* as you describe what he is doing.

Sort

Next look for groups. How can you divide the things into similar groups? Ask lots of questions and talk out loud as you are deciding how to group the objects. Be sure to use the word *sort* as you group the items. Include the whole family. Think together.

Choose

Finally, have each family member choose something from one of the groups. Once again, talk out loud as you tell each other why you chose that particular item. Remind everyone that they have just gathered, sorted, and chosen.

Children like to learn new concepts by doing things. They'll remember the phrase "Gather, Sort, and Choose" now that they've actually done it. You'll probably remember it better too.

Things for you to do

Now it's your turn to practice. But I'm going to have you work with ideas instead of things. Look back to the end of chapter 1 to see the idea you wanted to think about and the problem you wanted to solve. It may be helpful for you to write them down again.

the idea

■ _____

the Problem

■ _____

You're going to do some gathering, but you're just going to gather "inside information." You're only going to work with your own ideas.

■ Write down ten things you already know about your idea and ten possible solutions you already know to your problem. Write each idea on a small slip of paper or 3 x 5 index card.

■ Sort your ideas. Are some ideas similar? Put those slips of paper in the same pile. Look again. You may want to separate one large group into two smaller ones.

■ Choose your best two or three thoughts about your idea and your best two or three solutions to your problem. Save them. You'll look at them again later.

More things for your young Wisdom Thinker to do

■ Ask your child to go through the same process you just did for something she

wants to buy or something she wants to
do. If your child is having a lot of fun
with the activity, do both. Otherwise,
have her think only about buying or only
about doing.

I want to buy:

■ _____

I want to do:

■ _____

Now you and your child have had a concrete
experience of gathering, sorting, and choosing. And
you have worked with ideas. You've been thinking.
But you haven't used Wisdom Thinking yet. You
need to learn two more skills before good thinking
becomes Wisdom Thinking. Read on!

CHAPTER THREE

Skill Two:
Thinking about
Thinking

Jesus was an outstanding thinking-teacher. Being God, he understood the thoughts of both friends and enemies. He knew all about human minds and their imperfections. This knowledge gave him a unique opportunity to teach people how to think.

As we read different stories in the Gospels, we see Jesus dealing with many people who made choices without thinking about their thinking. The Pharisees are a prime example. Obeying the law was of utmost importance to them. They even added new laws to make sure they didn't disobey God's laws. But after years of lawmaking and law-following, they thought more about laws than about knowing God. When they tried to solve the problem, "Who is Jesus?" they could only answer that he was a man who didn't obey their many laws. Even when Jesus explained their blinded thinking, they wouldn't see the light (John 5:31-47).

Jesus' followers had trouble thinking about their thinking too. Martha and Mary solved the problem, "How do you act when Jesus comes to visit?" in different ways. Mary chose wisely. She sat and listened at Jesus' feet. Martha chose to be a perfect hostess. She bustled around making everything perfect. Martha became more and more upset when things weren't right for her guests. Jesus pointed out that all her preparations were not as important as listening to his words. Martha was only thinking about etiquette, which kept her from thinking wisely about what she should be doing (Luke 10:38-42).

Jesus tried to get Martha and the Pharisees to think about their thinking. He tried to help them think more about how they made their choices. We too can learn from what he taught. Wise thinkers think about their thinking.

Children as well as adults need to learn to think about their thinking. Does your child ever jump to conclusions because he doesn't take time to think? Does he sometimes act without thinking at all? Does he know how to make a plan to solve his problems? Or does he just start working on them haphazardly? Does he reconsider his choices after they're made? Or does he make the same mistakes over and over again? If he does any of these things, he needs to learn to think about his thinking.

When faced with a problem, Wisdom Thinkers do three things: First, they look ahead. They plan how they will gather, sort, and choose. Second, they keep a close eye on their thinking. They notice how they are doing and make changes when they need to. Third, they look back to see how well they did. Wisdom Thinkers learn from the thinking they have done.

LOOKING AHEAD TO THINKING

It's pie-making day. TAT, the plant manager, runs down her checklist before work begins. Are the workers ready to pick in the orchard? Does the conveyor belt run smoothly and at the right speed? Are knives sharpened and ready? Do the workers know what they're making today? As TAT walks through the factory, she makes sure the plant is ready to go.

Wisdom Thinkers plan ahead how they will think about an idea or make a decision before they gather, sort, and choose. They try to understand the problem they want to solve. And then they look forward by thinking carefully about their problem and how to do a good job solving it. At the same time, they plan how to avoid mind traps such as those that tripped up Martha and the Pharisees.

Understanding the Problem

Understanding the problem is the first step in looking ahead. It gets thinking started on the right track. This may sound simple, but many thinkers fail to find a good solution because problems aren't understood in the first place. In the factory, the workers must know if they're making pie or apple-sauce. Otherwise the end result may be pies filled with apple mush.

Understanding the problem is important because problems can be confusing for children. Annie said, "Rebecca hates me. She isn't my best friend anymore." To help Annie solve her friendship dilemma, a parent needs to help her understand what the problem is all about.

Simple questions can help. Simple questions are a thinker's best friend. If Annie were your child you might ask, "Why do you think she hates you? Did something happen to upset Rebecca? Did you ask her why she's mad?" When Annie understands the problem, she will have an idea of what she must do to solve it.

Having a Base of Knowledge

After understanding the problem, Wisdom Thinkers learn about the subject area in question. Annie needs to know more about the way children act and why they act that way. Some children act unfriendly when they are worried about problems at home. Or when they're not feeling well. Knowing more about behavior will help Annie evaluate Rebecca's actions.

If your teen is buying a car, he needs to know what a good quality car is like. If he's having problems with low grades, he needs to know his teacher's standards so he can work to raise his marks.

Twelve-year-old Tim believed children should be able to vote. But he knew nothing about voting except that he had to wait until he was eighteen to participate in an election. To help him examine his idea, his teacher suggested he find out what voters must know before casting ballots. Then Tim could decide if children were qualified to vote. Tim asked his parents what people must know before they vote. His mom showed him an old "Voter's Pamphlet." It was huge! But Tim decided to read through it anyway. Page after page, the candidates talked about budgets, expenditures, and arms control. Most of what they said was confusing. Tim didn't understand what they were talking about. He realized he didn't know who was right and who was wrong. So after enlarging his base of knowledge, Tim decided to leave voting to adults.

As your child grows older, his base of general knowledge will grow too. This is one of the reasons adults are able to make wiser decisions than children. It also explains why children have a harder time with complex problems. The more your child knows, the more "inside" information he has to work with. And it will be easier for him to gain helpful "outside" facts when he can think clearly about what he knows and what he still needs to learn.

Once a problem is understood, your child can move on to solve it. And the larger his base of knowledge about the problem area, the better his chances of making a wise choice.

Having a Thinking Plan

Wisdom Thinkers plan in advance how they will solve problems or investigate ideas. Without a plan, problem solving is like trying to get to a remote village in Alaska without a map and compass.

Have your child explain to you how he plans to think about his problem. Where is he going to gather information and why? If it's a moral question, is he going to look for answers in a teen magazine or ask a youth counselor? Ask him why one source is better than another.

How is he going to sort the information he gathers? If he's buying a tape player, is his main consideration price or quality? If he's buying clothes, what is his priority: to impress his friends or to please God?

When he's ready to make his choice, ask him to consider how his choice will affect himself and others. Help him to see how his choice will affect his character.

Planning Ahead to Avoid Mental Traps

Wisdom Thinkers plan ahead how they will avoid mental traps which sabotage wise thinking. The Pharisees were caught in the "little details" trap. Martha was caught in an "etiquette" trap. Being aware of traps and their potential for harm can help keep thinking moving ahead. Soldiers who know where land mines are buried have a better chance of getting across a field alive. Thinkers who know where mental traps lie have a better chance of making wise choices.

Some mental traps common among children are "smart people make the best choices" or "good thinkers are fast thinkers" and "there is only one way to solve a problem." If your child believes these myths, they will keep him from doing a good job thinking.

Wrong attitudes are also mental traps. Prejudice is a common attitude that hinders wise thinking. In John 1:45-46, Philip tells Nathanael that he's found the one Moses talks about in the Law—Jesus of Nazareth. Nathanael responds in disbelief, "Nazareth! Can anything good come from there?" If Nathanael had clung to his prejudice, he would never have met his Messiah.

Another attitude that hinders thinking is holding on too tight to tradition. Karen was a member of a club at high school. Every year the club held a bake sale to earn money for their activities. Karen noticed many other clubs held bake sales, and she wondered if they would do better with another kind of fundraiser. When she suggested it, the club president said no. Her reason for objecting was that it was a tradition to have bake sales every year. As Karen predicted, the sale generated little income.

Since thinking is an individual sport, the traps are different for each of us. Watch your child carefully. Is your daughter tripped by believing that only boys are good at math? Does your son believe only girls take music lessons? Does your child believe the only right way to exercise is the way the P.E. teacher says? Point out mental traps before they damage thinking.

Understanding the problem, having a base of knowledge and a thinking plan, and looking out for mental traps are good preparation for choosing what to believe or do. They take just a few minutes of thinking time, and they're worth every second.

KEEPING AN EYE ON THINKING

TAT watches as gatherers pick apples. She spots some workers picking unripe apples. One throws twigs and leaves into her bag. TAT tells them to gather carefully to help cut down on sorting later.

When the conveyor belt begins to roll, sorters move into place. TAT watches as they grab out those apples that won't be useful. One tired worker lets bad apples roll by. TAT suggests he take a rest. Another worker works too fast. TAT gets him to slow down. During baking, TAT checks the ovens. Pies that are doughy when they emerge from the ovens are sent back for more baking. Burnt pies are thrown out. TAT feels rewarded when the pies are just right.

Wisdom Thinkers think about their thinking during every step of gathering, sorting, and choosing. The goal of Wisdom Thinking is not just to find any old answer. It is to find the best possible answer. Keeping an eye on thinking helps produce better choices. Keeping an eye on thinking improves our understanding of ideas.

There are many ways to think about thinking while gathering, sorting, and choosing. The more your child is aware of how she thinks, the better thinking can be. Knowing three "Fs" of thinking about thinking will help: *focus* on the problem, be *fair-minded,* and realize how *feelings* affect thinking.

Focus on the Problem

A photographer prepares to take a close-up picture. He zooms in to focus on the subject he wants to capture. Everything else blurs into the background. Wisdom thinkers do the same when solving a problem or investigating an idea. They focus on the subject before them. The landscape around them becomes less important.

Keeping their goal in sight, they set out to reach it. The path to their goal is gathering, sorting, and choosing. By keeping their feet on the path and their eyes on the goal ahead, they are able to get to the end more directly. They're not easily sidetracked or distracted.

My daughter, Sarah, loved math until her class started long division in fourth grade. It stumped her. Suddenly she hated one of her favorite subjects. She was so frustrated she turned off all help aimed in her direction. Having given up, her mind wandered during math time.

Alerted by a lower-than-usual grade on a math test, I realized the only way she was going to improve was by focusing on her problem. So we sat down and worked on long division day after day. Freed from school distractions, Sarah was able to catch at home what had escaped her at school. Focusing on her problem helped solve her "problems."

Fair-mindedness

Fair-mindedness is being willing to listen, to spend time thinking, and to respect the opinions of others. Fair-minded thinkers are not impulsive or out to prove their point. They want to understand. They don't have to come up with the best idea or win every argument. Inquisitive and interested in the world around them, these thinkers are learners.

Fair-minded thinkers double-check information before they act on it. They sort carefully, giving each fact or idea full attention. They work with each option to see its merits. Even if it's not usable this time, they may learn something that will help next time. Fair-minded thinkers choose honestly.

Gail wanted to paint the walls of her room fire-engine red, a color that nauseated her mom. So Gail's mom took her to the paint store and asked her to select at least ten colors she might like. Gail agreed. For two weeks Gail combined and matched paint chips. She considered her mom's opinion. Finally Gail picked a color they both liked, and accented her room with fire-engine red.

Gail was helped to be fair-minded by the example of her mom. And she ended up with a nice-looking room. After taking time to look at many options, she agreed that softer colors were more restful. Together Gail and her mom generated a new idea instead of fighting over who was right and who was wrong.

Feelings Affect Thinking

How your child feels about himself. Stephen rushed by his mother without a hello. She could tell by the scowl on his face that something was wrong. Seconds later his little brother Paul walked in and said quietly, "Stephen and I had a fight and he won't play with me anymore." Mom sighed. Stephen was having a hard time dealing with his emerging and raging hormones. On good days, his problems were microscopic. On bad days, they were bigger than Godzilla. It was a Godzilla day, for sure.

Feelings have a place in the thinking process. But helping kids see through emotionally distorted problems is a tough challenge for parents. Though there's no magic solution, there are a few common-sense things you can do:

1. Prepare yourself and your child. Begin thinking training long before emotions are the big issue.

2. Work hard to keep communication lines open. Be there to listen and talk.

3. Share about your own ups and downs. Let her know she's not alone.

4. Remember, it won't last forever.

Tracy's main feeling was a need for acceptance by her friends, especially Jody, the most popular girl at school. Tracy was a good thinker—she knew right from wrong—but she felt like a puppet. Whenever Jody pulled her strings, Tracy did what she was told.

Fortunately, intense peer pressure doesn't last forever either. But, as strong as hormones can be, the need for acceptance can be stronger. It can override even the best thinker's intentions. So how does a parent deal with feelings of peer pressure? With limits on behavior, plenty of patience, understanding, and a lot of preparation. Begin "thinking training" early before your child's peers become his authorities. Teach your child to evaluate sources before peers have their greatest say.

How your child feels about thinking. Kim has healthy feelings about thinking. She is excited to try her hand at making choices. When difficult problems arise, she sees them as a challenge rather than an obstacle. Some children grow up like Kim believing thinking is fun. Those children are more likely to work at being better thinkers.

Kim is also a flexible thinker. She's learned that good thinking involves change. Giving up an old idea to gain a new and better one makes sense to her. A teacher told her once that old ideas are like scruffy, well-worn slippers. We get attached to them and resist throwing them out even though they no longer keep our feet warm. But if we need warm feet, the slippers have to go. Kim is willing to let go of old ideas. She's learned to be flexible when it comes to thinking.

Greg doesn't share Kim's feelings about thinking. From the time he was small, he learned to fear thinking failures. His family often told him he was dumb, and now Greg feels dumb. Even though his grades are good, Greg doesn't raise his hand in class very often. His papers lack imagination. He never had the freedom to fail, and now it keeps him from being a wise thinker.

Feelings about thinking begin at home. Kim grew up in a healthy thinking environment where she could practice her new thinking skills without fear. Greg wasn't so fortunate. Your child's feelings about thinking make a great difference in what she can accomplish.

By keeping an eye on thinking, your child can uncover and correct problems she encounters when gathering, sorting, and choosing. If careful thinking has been practiced, a better choice should result. But choosing isn't the end of thinking. There is a little more work to be done.

LOOKING BACK AT THINKING

In the apple pie factory, TAT checks the pies when they're done She looks for clues to what went well and what didn't. Pie filling that tastes bad points to picking and sorting problems. Burnt crusts indicate baking failure. Making notes, TAT prepares for the next day's work. Because she looked back, better pies should result.

A choice has been made, an idea has been investigated, the job is almost finished. Now your child needs to look back and rate how well thinking was performed. This can be done by asking two questions. Did I solve my problem? What did I learn?

Carrie asked these two questions after she chose to go to Ten Acres Bible Camp. The camp was fun, and she met some nice friends. So it solved her problem about what to do for a summer activity. But she learned that she hadn't read the brochure very carefully. If she had, she would have realized Ten Acres didn't have horses, which she wanted to learn to ride. The camp she had attended the year before did have horses. Next year she'd go back to the other camp.

These are simple questions, but they'll expose a faulty thinking plan. They'll reveal if an eye strayed away from the thinking path. And these two questions will force your child to look back at his thinking. Then thinking about thinking will begin to be a habit.

Taking a Second Look Back

Most choices aren't carved in stone, but often people act as though they are. We're not failures if we go back and choose again, like Carrie. That's part of being fair-minded. Maybe at some later date, new ideas or facts can come to light. These new ideas may make old choices undesirable. And if we made an unwise choice, it's in our own best interest to make a change for the better.

Teach your child to reconsider old choices, but don't make him anguish over the past. Encourage him to look back now and again at old solutions. Help him decide if a rethink is in order.

Thinking about thinking is a vital element of investigating ideas and solving problems. It is a safeguard which helps the thinker use his thinking machine wisely. Combined with gathering, sorting, and choosing, better decisions result.

Keep building on those concepts you've practiced during the last two chapters. If you didn't try them, it's never too late. Go back and do them now. Thinking about thinking will make more sense if you apply it to your own life.

YOU TRY IT!

Things for you to do

You've just learned how to think about your thinking. Now for some practice.

It's time to remember your idea from the chapter 1 activities. Think back to that problem you wanted to solve. When you think about your thinking remember just three things: Look ahead, look back, and while you're in the middle, keep looking. This time you're going to work with "outside" information. You're going to gather from people and print. For this practice don't gather too much. Talk with one or two people and read two or three things. Let's get started.

Look ahead. Make a plan. Where are you going to get "outside" information? Who are you going to talk to and what are you going to read? Your plan can be long and detailed or short and general. The most important thing is that you do have a thinking plan.

Keep looking. So now you have a plan. And you're busy gathering that "outside" information. Soon you'll be sorting it. Are you being fair-minded? For example, if you're investigating abortion, are you finding out about both prochoice and prolife?

How about emotions? Are they surging so that you can't think clearly about your idea or problem? Ask yourself how your emotions are affecting your gathering, sorting, and choosing. Make a change if you need to.

Look back. Now that you're done gathering and sorting, choose your two best ideas. Choose your two best solutions to your problem. Now look back. Did you solve the problem you set out to solve? Did you investigate your original idea? Or did you get side-tracked? How could you have improved your thinking plan?

Things for your young Wisdom Thinker to do

Help your son or daughter through the process of thinking about thinking. Teach him to look ahead, look back, and while he's in the middle, to keep on looking. Remember, it's time to gather "outside" information. Teach your child what you just learned.

Now you and your child have learned to gather, sort, and choose. And you've learned to think about your thinking. This is almost Wisdom Thinking. We have to add one more skill before your good thinking becomes Wisdom Thinking. We have to think about God.

CHAPTER FOUR

Skill Three: Thinking about God

It was the end of another long day in the desert wilderness. God's wandering people were thirsty. And they complained—loudly. Always compassionate, Yahweh heard their cries for help. He told Moses how to meet their need in the barren land. "Speak to that rock and it will pour out its water."

The Lord's instructions were clear. But after forty long years with a grumbling crowd of nomads, Moses was fed up with their behavior. In fact, he was so angry when he stood before them that he roared, "Listen you rebels, must we bring you water out of this rock?" Raising his staff, he struck the boulder twice and water flowed.

Moses was the hero of the day. He solved the water shortage problem. But in the process, he made a terrible thinking error. He failed to think about God and his instructions. God told Moses to speak to the rock, not to hit it. And as a result of this one refusal to honor God in the presence of his people, Moses wasn't allowed to enter the promised land (Numbers 20:2-12).

Moses learned the hard way. Problems can be solved without *thinking about God,* but they are best solved thinking his way. Your child must learn to include God in her gathering, sorting, and choosing. When she has a problem, she needs to learn from God's Word, listen to wise counselors, and lean on God in prayer. Thinking About God will make the difference between good thinking and Wisdom Thinking.

> The fear of the LORD is the beginning of
>   wisdom,
> and knowledge of the Holy One is under-
>   standing.
>
> Proverbs 9:10

LEARNING FROM GOD'S WORD

It's been said that most Christians in America have more light than they're willing to walk in. That's true. We have thousands of churches where Bible truths are preached every week, twenty-four-hour radio and television programs that proclaim God's Word, and Christian books galore to browse through at our leisure. So why do so many believers fail to live faithful, Christian lives? God's Word isn't part of their day-to-day thinking and choice making.

Wisdom Thinkers use and obey God's Word. We must not only teach our children to use the newest information, they must also learn to depend on the ancient Bible to gain God's perspective. His point of view will guide their thinking as they gather and sort and choose. When a choice is made, it will be measured by the highest standard—the Word of God. Using the Bible throughout thinking will lead to wiser choices.

In the illustration of the apple pie factory, remember TAG (Thinking about God)? He's the one who holds the Recipe in his hands. As he watches the gathering and sorting of apples, he makes sure each piece of fruit meets the standard which will result in the best end product. He watches as the pies are put together. Are the proportions correct? Do the workers follow directions? When the pies are finished baking, TAG only allows pies which meet the Recipe's high standard to leave the factory.

Following the Recipe

The Wisdom Thinker's "secret family recipe" is the Bible. "All Scripture is God-breathed and is useful for teaching, rebuking, correcting and training in righteousness, so that the man of God may be thoroughly equipped for every good work" (2 Timothy 3:16-17).

Christians need to go to the Bible for help when making decisions about their lives. Direct commands are to be followed. Principles, such as the proverbs, give good advice. Examples from the lives of biblical characters provide encouragement to do good and warn against evil. When the recipe is followed, wise solutions result.

But how can you teach your child to look to the Bible for help and guidance?

Be a good example of Thinking About God from the time your child is small. From the time they were married, Anne and Steve made a habit of doing their personal Bible reading in the family room. When the kids were small, they simply explained the Bible helped them solve problems. As the children grew older, they explained a little about their problem, what passages they were reading, and what they had learned to apply to their lives.

When your child has a problem to solve or an idea to investigate, lead her to the Word. Anne and Steve's children learned by watching their parents' example. They would often come to their mom and dad, Bible in hand, asking where to find help for their problems. They looked up the passages together and decided what choices their child could make. Other families have to instigate Bible problem solving. If your child doesn't think of using the Word when she has a dilemma, try sitting down together when there are few distractions. Find helpful passages that are familiar to you, or look in a topical Bible to locate passages which address the area of concern. Read them together.

Read about Christians who used the Bible to make choices. The Baker family began reading missionary stories and biographies when their children were in grade school. They've learned about Hudson Taylor obeying Jesus' command to spread the gospel by starting China Inland Mission. Corrie Ten Boom's story, *The Hiding Place,* taught them all about obedience and bravery when the Ten Booms chose to hide Jews in their home during World War II. And they've followed the life and ministry of Joni Eareckson Tada who used God's Word to make many difficult choices after a diving accident left her paralyzed. If your family likes real-life stories, visit your local Christian bookstore and pick up some of the biographies and missionary stories which teach wise thinking through example. You can read these as a family or tell these stories to your child.

Solve "pretend problems" together. Tom and Kathy have a family night each week. Sometimes they just have silly fun. But other nights they have more serious conversations. One "game" their children enjoy is, "What would you do if . . ." They solve pretend problems together. If your family is willing, use this method with your children too. Go step by step through gathering, sorting, and choosing, all the while Thinking about Thinking, and especially Thinking about God. Place priority on choosing God's way.

Doing these things will highlight Thinking about God. Each will foster a positive attitude toward God's Word and its value in thinking. But just having a good attitude about the Bible is not enough to use it fully. And that leads us to the need for Bible knowledge.

Understanding the Recipe

Workers in the pie factory have to understand the directions in the recipe in order to make pies that meet the quality standard each and every time they bake. The same is true for Wisdom Thinkers. They need to know God's Recipe and understand it in order to make good choices time and time again.

God's Word is meant to be read and understood. But it is not a book of easy step-by-step answers like most self-help books written today. Compiled over fifteen hundred years, in several different styles, in three different languages, by various writers, the Bible is a complex book. It takes time to read and understand its message and its teachings. But the fact that Thinking About God is at the heart of Wisdom Thinking makes knowledge and understanding of God's Word a top priority for all Christians, adults and children alike.

Parents must teach their children to use the Bible when thinking. How?

First, teach your child to read the Bible.

These commandments that I give you today are to be upon your hearts. Impress them on your children. Talk about them when you sit at home and when you walk along the road, when you lie down and when you get up.

Deuteronomy 6:6-7

Until I became a Christian at sixteen, I never read the Bible outside of church on Sunday. My knowledge of Bible events was limited to sketchy Sunday school lessons. As a result, upon entering Multnomah School of the Bible at nineteen, I had a lot to learn. I thought I was doing okay until I entered a class on the Book of Acts with Dr. John Mitchell. There, even the best students found out how little they really knew. He asked countless questions we students couldn't answer, and each time Dr. Mitchell came back with his lilting Scottish reply, "Don'cha read yer Bibles?"

John Mitchell taught us the value of Bible reading. He knew from years of experience that countless Bible classes could not substitute for time spent reading and meditating on God's written Word. Verses that were "obscure" to us were his well-known friends, they were part of his life and thinking. He wanted us to see the Bible in the same way.

You can help your child make the Bible part of his thinking through Bible reading. Do this by reading the Bible together, and encouraging him to read on his own. As early as possible, add a readable modern translation to his library. Noel and I recommend these two:

The Adventure Bible: A Study Bible for Kids (Zondervan) contains the New International Version. Written at a seventh-grade reading level, it has a dictionary, concordance, and many study helps.

The International Children's Bible (Word) is a fourth-grade reading level translation with many pictures, a dictionary, and maps.

Reading Bible stories is helpful too. But be sure you also look up the story reference in a Bible and read it the way it was written. Some Bible story books include questions to help your child understand the text. This is a great approach.

Remember, your child will be watching to see if you read your Bible, too. You will be his model of how Christian adults behave. Wisdom Thinkers read their Bibles and know them well.

Second, teach your child to understand the Bible. This is where many Christians jump ship when dealing with God's Word. It's easier to have someone else tell us what the Bible says (like our pastor) than to take the time to learn how to study the Bible ourselves. But most of us do not have an expert in biblical studies on call to guide us through our day-to-day decisions. Therefore, the choices we make are based on our own understanding of the Bible. If we understand it well, we make better choices.

Teach your child to study the Bible as he grows. Understanding the different types of literature, how to do cultural and word studies, and recognizing the difference between commands, principles, and promises can greatly increase your child's ability to interpret God's Word.

Third, teach your child to use the Bible in his own thinking. Mandy and her brother, Will, fought daily over who should get the most time on the family computer. When Mandy and Will went to their mother asking for help, she suggested they gather, sort, and choose. Mandy wrote down the reasons she wanted to use the computer. This was her list: it's fun, I can practice math problems, I'm learning states and capitals. Then Will listed his reasons. He wrote: I write reports on the word processor, I like to play Flight Simulator, I practice math problems.

Then the three of them went to the Bible to look up passages which would help solve their problem. Most of the passages they read talked about relationships. Mandy and Will were reminded about how people who love each other behave. First Corinthians 13:4-7 was especially helpful. They both admitted they were more concerned about getting their own way than working out a good solution.

Now that Mandy and Will had a better attitude, they sorted the needs and wants on their lists in order of importance. Will's reports were important;

so was Mandy's math practice. Will's math wasn't suffering, he just liked to play with numbers. Mandy felt the same about the states and capitals. As for the games, they were the last priority.

When it came time to choose a solution, they agreed to allow time each day for the biggest needs. Then, when both were done with their primary computer need, they could divide up the time left for more fun time.

For Will and Mandy, the Bible is an indispensable tool for Wisdom Thinking. Teach your child to trust in this tool too. Keeping biblical commands, examples, and principles in mind throughout thinking keeps Wisdom Thinking on track.

LISTENING TO WISE COUNSELORS

Proverbs tells us there is another source God uses to guide his children.

Listen to advice and accept instruction,
and in the end you will be wise.

Proverbs 19:20

Instruct a wise man and he will be wiser
still;
teach a righteous man and he will add to
his learning.

Proverbs 9:9

How do you picture a wise person? Sitting alone on a mountain top, gray beard flowing to the ground? Or walking through a palace, aides trailing behind, doing her every bidding? Toss out those images. According to Solomon, the wise person listens to counselors, recognizes good advice, and takes it. Wise people know they don't know everything. But they're always willing to learn.

In the apple pie factory, TAG asks advice from professional consultants. He wants his factory to run smoothly. He realizes outside observers can spot problems he hasn't seen.

Teach your child to make use of wise counselors by being a good example yourself. Let him know that you ask others for guidance. Paula, a mother of two, adopted an older couple from her church growth group, Helen and Ralph, as surrogate parents for herself and grandparents for her children. After struggling through several years of difficult family problems, she realized the need for caring input from some older and wiser Christians. Though Ralph and Helen had children of their own, they recognized Paula's need for them in her life. Now Paula's children are seeing first-hand how wise counselors can be an important part of thinking and choosing.

Paula chose her wise counselors well. Ralph is an elder in their church, and Helen is a down-to-earth, loving, mature Christian. Both are respected for their godly character, integrity, and wisdom. In addition, they are older than Paula, and are able to give her the benefit of their years of practice in making decisions.

Choosing Wise Counselors

All of us need wise counselors. Some of us go to church leaders for professional help, but other wise church members can help us through those daily life questions we wouldn't want to bother the pastor with. But how do we find these wise counselors?

If your church has growth groups or other small discussion groups, women's Bible studies, men's prayer breakfasts, or community outreach programs, these are ideal places to mix with adults of all ages. Don't limit your church activities to those which only involve people your own age. Go to retreats and sit with the older generation too. Meet them in Sunday school, on church workdays, in committee meetings, or serving in the nursery.

Listen to what they have to say. Watch the reactions of those around them. Whom do others appear to respect? Once you've met them, let your appreciation for their wisdom show. Ask their opinion and listen carefully to their answers. Work on building a relationship. Ask them to lunch, over for dinner, out for a walk. Pretty soon you'll find you have the help you need.

Finding a wise counselor is the key to getting good advice. Not everyone qualifies for the job. Help your child find wise people like Ralph and Helen. Look to your extended family, friends from church, Christian teachers, neighbors, and coaches. Help your child develop friendships early in his life with people who can counsel him during his teens when he might be less likely to listen to you. Children who have a network of wise counselors to choose from have a better chance of using this type of resource.

Gathering and Sorting with Wise Counsel

When your child has a problem to solve, have him gather ideas from more than one counselor. This is the same idea as gathering facts widely, which we discussed in chapter 2. Getting more than one perspective on a problem will help him develop balance and discernment.

My children often discuss problems with their grandmothers. Sometimes Sarah and Josh hear the same advice from Grandma and Nana that they hear from my husband and me. When that happens, the added reinforcement sometimes helps them make good choices. Other times, these wise women give my kids new ways to think about their problem. Sarah or Josh often tell us that new idea, and we discuss it together. I appreciate the greater perspective grandmothers give. They often suggest creative solutions to my children's problems, solutions I never would have thought of!

Choosing Wisely

Many people go to counselors for advice hoping the counselor will tell them what to do. They want someone else to make choices for them. But that is not the responsibility of a wise counselor. And as a wise counselor, it's not good for parents to choose all the time for their children. But it isn't easy to sit by and watch. I know. I'm still learning to stop myself from making many choices my kids could make for themselves. During the sorting stage, counselors can advise which solution might work better than others. But in the end, the choice should often be left up to your child. Learning to live with choices is a part of maturing and growing in wisdom.

LEANING ON GOD IN PRAYER

If any of you lacks wisdom, he should ask God, who gives generously to all without finding fault, and it will be given to him.

James 1:5

Asking help from the Wisest Counselor is a never-to-be-forgotten element of thinking. The Holy Spirit is there to guide those who ask him for wisdom.

How does it work? How does the thinker know God is directing his thoughts? Will his stomach do flip-flops? Will he hear a voice saying, "Ask out the girl in the green shirt—she's my choice for you"? I don't think so. Not most of the time.

Dr. Ed Goodrick, in his book *Is My Bible the Inspired Word of God?,* explains that the Holy Spirit works so "skillfully that we are not even conscious of what he is doing and so manipulates our thought processes that his interpretations make sense to us." That is not to say that God never works in miraculous ways. But most often when we ask him for help, he takes what we have gathered and sorted and, if we allow him, reveals the best choices by helping us to think as he does. Then it is up to us to make that choice.

One evening Josh was upset when he and I sat down to pray before he went to bed. He had been having bad dreams for several nights in a row. Each night he had prayed God would keep him from having more nightmares. But each night the same scary dreams returned. When Josh prayed, he asked God why he didn't answer his prayers.

We talked afterward, and I explained that sometimes God says no to our requests. Josh wondered why God would do that. "God has reasons for answering our prayers in ways we sometimes don't understand," I explained. Josh thought for a moment. Then he said, "I think God wanted to teach me not to watch movies that I know are bad for me." Then he told me about a small part of a typical teen horror flick he'd seen at a friend's house. We prayed again. He slept soundly that night.

Prayer is not a substitute for gathering and sorting. Because we pray doesn't mean we don't need to think about thinking. Prayer isn't a substitute for reading God's Word and seeking wise counsel. But combined with these elements of wise thinking, prayer makes good choices possible.

Now try applying the last of the three skills to the ideas and problems you've been working on since chapter 1. There's still time to go back and start these activities if you skipped them. If you've done them, good for you! You're getting a good grasp on what you'll be teaching your child for the next few years.

YOU TRY IT!

Things for you to do

So that's it. Thinking about God is the third and final skill of Wisdom Thinking. As you think, remember to Read the Bible, Ask Wise Counselors, and Pray to God for Wisdom. Now for some more practice. Dust off that idea from chapter 1, and remember that old problem. If you were using Wisdom Thinking from the start, you would have been thinking about God when you first started your work back in chapter 2. But I thought it would be easier for you to learn the skills one at a time.

Read the Bible. What does the Bible say about your idea? Can you find any principles to help with your problem? Think of the words related to your idea or your problem. Look them up in the back of your Bible or in a concordance. Do some reading. What does God have to say?

Ask Wise Counselors. Does your church have elders? Some churches choose elders who exemplify godly qualities in their lives. These people walk with God; they are wise counselors. Even if your church doesn't have these kinds of elders you probably recognize those people who live lives pleasing to God. Talk to them about your idea. Ask them about your problem. Once again, be fair-minded and listen carefully.

Pray to God for Wisdom. If you had been practicing Wisdom Thinking back in chapter 1 you would have taken the time to pray to God as you thought about an idea to investigate. In chapter 2 you would have asked God to help you as you gathered and sorted and chose. And in chapter 3 you would have prayed to God for Wisdom as you made your thinking plan and as you tried to be fair-minded. Thinking about God affects the thinking process from beginning to end. Ask God for wisdom now as you come to the end of your thinking process. Do you understand the idea better? Have you solved the problem?

Things for your young Wisdom Thinker to do

Now help your child to think about God. Teach her to Read, Ask, and Pray. Now that your child has finished Wisdom Thinking, has she chosen something she would like to do? Has he picked something he wants to buy? If the choices are reasonable, now would be a good time to go ahead and act on them. That would be a nice way to end this introduction to Wisdom Thinking.

You and your child have learned to gather, sort, and choose. And you've learned to think about your thinking. You've even learned to think about God. This is Wisdom Thinking, and it takes practice to put it all together. In the next few pages watch Nina tackle an idea using Wisdom Thinking. She's been practicing her thinking for several years now. She's becoming wise.

Putting It All Together

You're now familiar with the three skills of Wisdom Thinking. You've learned all about gathering, sorting, and choosing. You know what it means to think about your thinking. And you know what it means to think about God.

But how does it all fit together? How is Wisdom Thinking used to investigate ideas or solve problems? Perhaps the individual skills look to you like musical instruments lying quietly in their cases. How can these separate instruments come together and play beautiful music? Nina will show you how. As this high school senior investigates an idea using Wisdom Thinking, you'll see how the three skills work together to form a whole thinking process.

(Whenever Nina uses a skill, it will be noted in parentheses. Thinking about Thinking will be designated by the letters "TAT." Thinking about God will be noted by the letters "TAG.")

Nina's Story

Nina's close friend, Alicia, got pregnant last year. She decided to keep her baby. Nina believes Alicia made the right choice, but others disagree. Now Nina wants to understand the three main options open to pregnant teens: She remembered that Mrs. Walsh next door adopted a baby from a teen mother, another girl friend of Nina's had an abortion, and Alicia chose parenthood. Nina would like to understand the pros and cons of teen parenthood, adoption, and abortion (*TAT—Understanding the Problem*). Asking for God's guidance, she begins her investigation (*TAG—prayer*).

First, Nina decides to find out more about teen pregnancy (*TAT—Base of Knowledge*). She reads about teens who have had babies. Some chose to become pregnant, others got pregnant by mistake. She learns why some chose abortions, others kept their babies, and others chose adoption.

Nina thinks about what she already knows about each of the three choices (*Gathering—Inside Information*). She believes abortion is the killing of a person and is therefore wrong. But it's also embarrassing being pregnant when you're not married, and raising a child on your own isn't easy. But giving a baby away seems almost impossible. Nina realizes she has strong opinions, but not many facts (*TAT—Mental Traps*).

So she begins to plan how she will investigate the three ways to deal with teenage pregnancy (*TAT—Thinking Plan*).

It will be important to fully understand abortion, adoption, and teen parenthood. To gather information she'll need to read about each option, and she'll need to listen to people who know about abortion, adoption, and teen parenting. She'll also need to evaluate her sources of information.

Nina writes down the places she'll go for information. She'll read her Bible, of course. Her youth group leader talked about abortion not long ago, so she'll ask him about it. She'll talk to her friend who had an abortion. Perhaps the Christian bookstore has some books that will answer some of her questions. The local library should have magazine and newspaper articles which will help. The subject intrigues her, and she spends hours thinking about it (*TAT—Focusing on the Problem*).

Nina tells her parents what she is doing and asks for their advice (*TAG—Wise Counselors*). She tells them why she feels she couldn't give a baby up for adoption. She can't imagine how any mother could (*TAT—Feelings*). But her parents point out that Mrs. Walsh is a good mother and that her child is happy. Nina agrees (*TAT—Fair-mindedness*).

Nina begins her gathering process (*Gathering—Outside Information*). At the bookstore she finds some books on teen pregnancy. One book talks about alternatives to abortion, the other is about teen parents. She buys and reads these two books.

Talking with her neighbor, Nina discovers that Mrs. Walsh loves Adam, her adopted child, as much as she loves Tina, her biological daughter. The adoptive mother feels that God gave her Adam, just as he gave her Tina. God just used another method when he gave her Adam.

One Sunday at church, Nina talks with Pat Richards who is active in the anti-abortion protest movement. Pat invites Nina to come and observe a meeting. Nina goes and gathers new facts and opinions about abortion from their literature. She also gathers information from those attending.

Nina asks Alicia if she would make the same choice to keep her baby if she had it to do all over again. Alicia thinks hard. She finally says she might have considered adoption if she had known how difficult raising a baby alone would be.

Nina meets with her youth group leader (*TAG—Wise Counselors*), and they discuss Bible passages that were part of his preparation (*TAG—Bible Study*). He gives her suggestions about other passages to read, and they pray together (*TAG—Prayer*).

At home Nina reads the Bible passages (*TAG—Bible reading*), and then she and her father look up the verses in two Bible commentaries (*TAG—Wise Counselors*). Most are about murder and punishment for sin. Some are about God taking caring of his people.

Nina has almost concluded her gathering. She wonders if she has missed any possible sources (*TAT—Fair-mindedness*). Thinking of her friend who had an abortion, she calls her. Nina talks with her about her reasons for going ahead with the abortion. Her friend still believes it was the right choice, although thinking about her abortion makes her sad.

Satisfied she has gathered well, Nina moves on to sorting.

Weeding through all the material and opinions takes time (*Sorting*), and Nina knows better than to rush (*TAT—Avoiding Mental Traps*). She keeps notes. First she writes down the major arguments for and against each option. Under each argument, she notes the people she talked to who support that position. She lists the articles she read. She also makes a list of priorities. God's commands and principles are first. Next she lists those ideas which aren't clearly right or wrong.

When Nina looks at her page on pros and cons about abortion, she is convinced it is not an option she agrees with. God condemns murder in his commandments. Those people on her list who support abortion are not concerned with obeying God's law. Nina is. She rejects abortion as an option open to pregnant teens (*Sorting*).

Her lists on the pros and cons of adoption and teen parenting grow longer. Teen parenting now looks harder than she had imagined when she began her investigation. Some of the facts she uncovered confirm that teen parenting often does not provide a secure life for the baby. As hard as adoption would be, Nina is now convinced that it would be best for the baby in most cases (*Choosing*). She decides it would depend on the parents and their families. Neither keeping the baby nor giving it up would be absolutely right or absolutely wrong.

Nina reviews the thinking she has done (*TAT—Looking Back*) and recognizes she has gained new understanding about a difficult issue. Now clear in her mind, Nina feels able to help friends who might find themselves pregnant and unmarried.

Young thinkers like Nina can make these kinds of informed investigations using Wisdom Thinking skills. In Nina's case, she chose to investigate an idea. But, if she had been pregnant, her Wisdom Thinking process would have led her to a wise choice.

Now read on to find out how to teach these skills to your child. The next section will help to show you how. Whatever your child's age, she can begin to learn to be a Wisdom Thinker like Nina.

Section Two

Your Child
and
Wisdom Thinking

CHAPTER FIVE

A Wise Thinker Grows

When my children were very small, check-ups at the pediatrician's office were a big event. In walked the nurse and off came my baby's clothes. Out came the scales and the tape measure. The inches, pounds, and ounces were pencilled in on the growth chart. Those little marks compared my baby to the normal growth of an "average child." I always wondered where the dots would lie that month. Would my baby be above average? Below? Somewhere in the middle?

When the nurse was done, Dr. Brody made his entrance. He checked ears, nose, throat, lungs, heart, and hips. We discussed my baby's development:

cooing, grabbing, sitting up, crawling, walking, and talking. The growth charts were analyzed. After a shot or two, we were sent home, assured that we were "doing fine." What a relief!

Most moms and dads are aware of the physical changes they can expect to take place as their child grows. We know tiny babies grow almost overnight. Soft little boy faces suddenly sprout scratchy whiskers. The cuddly toddler who once liked to sit on laps will soon run laps with her track team. Yet some of the most extraordinary changes a child experiences cannot be seen. Dramatic mental growth is keeping pace with physical growth. Parents need to understand these "inside" changes like they understand the physical changes. They need to know what changes to expect, and when to expect them.

Jon and Eric shared a room until Jon left home for college. One year later, Eric moved out. Now when mom walks by the empty room, she still remembers the early days when the floor was littered with match-box cars, Legos, crayons, and dozens of pieces of assorted toys. It seems so quiet. When the boys were small, the room resounded with yelling, giggling, and jumping on the bed. As they grew older, Jon spent more time reading. Eric played sports. It was good they had different interests because they fought like crazy whenever they were in the room together. The only thing they had in common was building model cars which replaced the match-box versions. Now when they come home, things are calmer. They spend hours together fixing up Eric's old Chevy he bought with money from his first job. And when they come home for a visit, they still share the same old room. But quiet talk has replaced bouncing on the bed—most of the time.

Even if your child is still small, you've already seen some incredible changes take place. Your child's changes, like Jon and Eric's, will continue into adulthood. We're going to look at some of these general changes to see how they affect thinking. Of course, children don't always follow the general patterns. Some children jump ahead, others lag behind. So we'll tell you about the general patterns, but we'll talk about some individual differences too.

This information will help you know what Wisdom Thinking skills to teach to your child at what age. You'll be able to make the most of changes in her development, and you'll get some idea of what lies ahead for your child's mental development.

MEET GERTIE GATHERER : EARLY CHILDHOOD (BEFORE AGE SIX)

Gertie and her friends are known by lots of names: preschoolers, rug rats, tykes. And we're giving them a new name—we're going to call them *gatherers* because that's what they do most. They do some simple sorting, and they make some choices, but mostly Gertie and her friends gather information. Gatherers are new at the business of thinking. They have little "inside" knowledge. So they spend their waking hours grabbing up bits of information.

To help your gatherer, it is important to reduce Wisdom Thinking to it's simplest form. We don't expect her to master all the skills of Wisdom Thinking. She's just starting out. She'll do best when learning a small skill here and a small skill there. So plan to relax and have fun. It will be a long time before she will begin to put the skills together to make them work as a whole. But this is the time to get started. These few guidelines will help to build her gathering skill.

Keep it simple. Little children need simple things to think about. They need simple choices to make. So when you're helping her to learn to think, give just a couple of instructions at a time. Too often I made the mistake of saying something like, "Go to your room, pick up your shoes, put them in the closet, and put your toys in the box in the living room." Then my child would look at me and say, "Huh?" Don't make my mistake of asking your gatherer to do too many things at once. She will learn better if you ask her to choose to do only one or two things each time. Then have her do her choice of things over and over again until she's good at doing those tasks.

Keep it short. Attention spans are short in this age group. Gertie gets tired after ten or fifteen minutes of the same activity. When working or playing, she likes variety. You'll notice she needs something new to do often or she gets bored. If you have a child Gertie's age let her move on to new thinking activities frequently.

Keep it active. If you're a worn-out parent of a preschooler, you don't need anyone to tell you that your child enjoys being active! There's a good reason for this. Gatherers actually get more tired when forced to sit for long periods of time. Their bodies are made for active learning, and you can use this to your advantage. Thinking can be taught through play. Gather, sort, and choose while you're building a fantastic Lego spacemobile or playing house or pretending you're at school. Talk about gathering, sorting, and choosing while you're doing these kinds of things together. It's fun and effective to teach thinking using games and toys.

Emphasize gathering. Gatherers will do all aspects of Wisdom Thinking, but emphasize gathering—it's what comes naturally. Gatherers go through the "What's that?" stage and the "Why?" stage. Try to answer these questions as much as possible. I remember wheeling my gatherers in a shopping cart through the produce section at the store, answering "What's that?" questions. "That's okra, sweetie. That's spinach, yum, yum. That's a turnip, that's squash, that's lettuce, that's corn. . . ." By the end of the shopping trip, I qualified as a vegetable too. But for my children, it was gathering, pure and simple.

We can help gatherers add to their knowledge by taking them to visit new places and new people. Free to explore and investigate, they'll gather on their own. Our role is to guide, rather than to teach in a structured way.

Keep it playful. Play is Gertie Gatherer's main activity. You can use play in all kinds of ways to teach thinking. You might like to try some of these suggestions:

> If your child plays in the sand or in water (even the bath tub), fill containers with her. Count how many little cups go into a big container. Then fill another container. Compare—which holds more?

> If you don't mind a mess, get out the paint box. Get a big piece of paper and drop

single spots of color on it. Let your child mix them together to make new colors. Most kids don't need any encouragement for this kind of gorpy activity. Or get out the clay or the finger paints. Let her feel the textures. What happens when they dry? Do they flake, crack, feel like a rock?

When she plays with other children, she will learn how other children react to her. Try starting some cooperative games. Though I'm not much of a "game person" myself, I've always admired the moms who could jump in and teach a game. But even I could organize "follow the leader." Maybe you're good at "Simon says."

Many kids like to play guessing games. Have her predict how many blocks can stack up before her tower collapses. Which cup has a rock hidden under it? How far can she throw a ball, a sock, a feather? Which will float—a piece of wood, a sponge, a Hot Wheels car?

All these types of play lead to discovery. Trial and error and experimentation teach thinking. Understanding the rules of the world will help her organize her knowledge as she grows older. Eventually, she will make wise decisions based on that knowledge. It may look like play—and it's certainly fun—but it's learning to think too.

MEET SAM SORTER : MIDDLE CHILDHOOD (AGES SIX TO TWELVE)

Sam has moved on from all that "little kid stuff." He still gathers, but now he's developing a new skill.

He's a *sorter.* Sorters like Sam are learning how to work with what they have gleaned. You can almost see the wheels turning inside their heads as they try to make sense of the information they possess. The following guidelines will help you understand your sorter.

Sorters learn from print. Gertie Gatherer's main source of information was objects—she learned by doing. Sam Sorter is beginning to learn from what he reads, hears, and sees. Still, he is no philosopher. His thinking is *concrete.* That means he understands best what he can see, hear, and feel.

The movement from being an active learner to a book learner is slow. If you have a younger sorter, he will still spend a large portion of his day in active play. As he grows, fewer hours will be devoted to that form of learning. Most sorters move on gradually to reading, talking, listening, and observing as they become more complex thinkers.

Sorters learn how to remember. Memory is an essential part of thinking. Remember the "inside" knowledge that Wisdom Thinkers depend on? That is memory. Sam Sorter's memory is becoming a useful tool. Developing a good recall of knowledge is vital to being a wise thinker in all areas of life. Kids from six to twelve test their memories every day at school as they complete assignments and take tests.

You can help your sorter develop her memory through any of these fun activities:

> Card and board games can be used to test recall (one is even called "Memory").
>
> My children enjoy hand-clapping poems done with a partner. There are so many new fun poems today. I can only

remember "Pease porridge hot, pease porridge cold, pease porridge in the pot, nine days old" from my childhood.

You might be familiar with that old string game, cat's cradle. It involves wrapping a string between your hands in many different configurations, then passing it to a partner. It promotes memory and dexterity at the same time.

Music is a wonderful memory tool. Many children enjoy singing while interpreting the song with American Sign Language.

Of course, Bible memorization is one of the best ways to exercise memory. One of my good friends puts Bible verses to song. Her children laugh at her silly tunes, but they sure remember the verses!

Don't be afraid to try anything that makes remembering easier for your child.

Sorters learn when to remember. Sorters also need to learn to be selective about what they remember. Some things don't have to be memorized to be remembered. The serial number from your child's bike can be written down for safekeeping. Telephone numbers can be looked up in a phone book. Other things should be forgotten. Sometimes talking over painful or scary experiences helps children to forget them. Understanding why a friend might say hurtful things might help your child not to dwell on those unkind words. Asking God to remove those words and images is always appropriate. Help your child learn what he needs to remember and what he needs to forget.

Sorters learn from experts and peers. You are still your sorter's king or queen of knowledge, though your crown will slip during these years. Try to maintain an openness so that he will continue to feel free to consult you. If we don't give our children the answers they need, they will go elsewhere.

Sam Sorter enjoys learning from experts. You might take him on a mini-field trip to learn about fighting fires from a fireman. Or have a farmer show you how a farm works. Many children get new insights on life by watching their parents work. Let him see how you think about your work and what choices you make. This is the time to help him learn at the front lines.

Your sorter is also learning from peers at school. When he is involved in group activities, watch how he interacts with his friends and other children. See if he responds well to them. Are there areas in which his social learning can be improved?

Emphasize sorting. Again, Sam Sorter can practice all Wisdom Thinking skills—he will still be gathering and choosing—but use this time to build on gathering and focus on sorting. You can try any or all of the following activities to help your sorter refine his sorting skills:

> Practice putting things back where they belong. Your child will begin to see that certain items belong in certain places. The salt and pepper shakers go on the stove, the dolls go on the shelf in her room, clean laundry goes in the drawer, dirty laundry goes in the hamper. Later she will match ideas to each other in the same way.

Group like items together. Look at pictures of animals on a farm. Some animals have four legs, others have two. Some animals have feathers, others have fur. Make groups for the animals. What group can all the animals belong to? What group can some of the animals belong to? Is there a group that none of the animals belongs to?

Work with the ideas of "bigger" and "smaller." The dad is bigger than the son. The mom is smaller than the dad. The son is bigger than the sister.

"Who or what does this come from?" Fred is my dad. I am Fred's daughter. Grandpa is Dad's father. Dad is Grandpa's son. Grandpa is Dad's boss. Dad is Grandpa's employee. Dad is Mom's husband.

Arrange facts by age or chronology. Who is the oldest in your family? Who is the youngest? What happened first, second, and third from the time your child got up this morning?

Mix the above sorting activities. Try using the people from the "Who or what does this come from?" activity (Fred, Grandpa, Mom) and group them like you did the animals. Group the people according to type. Who are the dads? Who are children? Who belongs to both groups? Which are children and are bigger? Which are mothers and are smaller? Which are members of both groups?

School is the main activity. School takes up about thirty hours per week of your sorter's time. Find out what your child is learning, especially about thinking. Look at his text books. Do you see ways he can apply the three skills of Wisdom Thinking to his class work? Is he learning about evolution in science? Perhaps a little TAG (Thinking about God) is in order. Observe how he does his homework. Does he gather, sort, and choose when he's working on reports? Help him apply his new skills to thinking inside school as well as at home.

MEET CHELSEA CHOOSER : ADOLESCENCE (AFTER AGE TWELVE)

Chelsea Chooser's life is full of choices. For years others have made decisions for her. Now suddenly she is making many choices on her own. What classes will she take in school? Who will be her friends? Who will she date? What clothes will she wear? Where will she go to college?

Most kids look forward to being independent thinkers and independent choosers. That's the fun part. The hard part is dealing with confusing changes and up-and-down emotions which make wise thinking more difficult. So your chooser needs your support to make the most of her teenage years. Help her to use Wisdom Thinking when she's feeling great and when she's feeling awful. You can help your chooser by doing any of the following things.

Work with ideas. Choosers have moved beyond the concrete world they can touch and see, into the world of ideas. They're ready to talk about broad concepts like truth, justice, and love. It's time to relate these ideas to everyday life. What is real friendship, true love, undying loyalty, senseless hate? How should she think about evolution, alternative lifestyles, new age music, and safe sex? What image does she convey to the world in her attitudes, style of dress, and form of communication?

How do the ideas she considers relate to God? Does God care about the way she chooses to live and think? How is she responsible for God's creation, including herself? What is God's place in planning her future?

Like Nina, the chooser in the last chapter, young people of this age can put all the skills of Wisdom Thinking together to investigate ideas. Help your child see that most issues have many sides. Help her exercise her gathering, sorting, and choosing. Challenge her to think about her own thinking. Focus on including thinking about God in her choices.

Work with symbols. Chelsea Chooser needs to learn to apply symbolic thinking to real-life experiences. Math is probably the most common example of this type of symbolic reasoning. Your child may know how to multiply A and B to equal C. But now she must apply that knowledge to solve life problems. How many monthly checks from her job at Burger King will it take to buy that car she so desperately wants? Teach her to solve real-life story problems.

In the same way, she must learn to apply rules of logic to her real-life thinking. Logical thinking says if a=b and b=c, then a=c. If my diet calls for one stalk of broccoli which has thirty-six calories, and there are thirty-six calories in one cup of chopped green onions, I can substitute green onions in my diet and not go over my calorie limit for the day. But, of course, it wouldn't be too logical to eat a cup of green onions before your first date with that special someone!

There are symbols in our language and culture that your child needs interpreted for her. When people make a "V" with their fingers, do they mean, "Victory," "Peace, brother," or "Live long and prosper"? What are people who drive Rolls Royces trying to say? When people use foul language, what image do they project?

Symbols are all around us. Help your chooser translate them into usable Wisdom Thinking.

Work with generalizations. A generalization is an idea that is most often true. The use of generalizations is an important step in transferring knowledge from one situation to another.

How do idea generalizations work? Suppose you grew up in a household with many dogs. You generalize that all dogs are nice. Each new dog you meet is treated with that confidence . . . until you meet Rambo. You reach down to pat Rambo and Rambo bites down on your arm. Now you know there is at least one exception to your rule. It is true that most dogs are nice, but not all. Not Rambo.

Children often consider generalizations to be facts when they have not seen exceptions. Chelsea Chooser needs to learn to use generalizations with care. She must know that most of the time these ideas are dependable, but sometimes she will have to change them when encountering new ideas.

There are also generalized ways of thinking. Wisdom Thinking is an example of a system that generally works well when transferred from one situation to the next. But, in an emergency, taking the time to go through all the steps of Wisdom Thinking may not be wise. If there's a fire, don't gather, sort, and choose. Get out of the building!

Emphasize choosing. Choosers, like gatherers and sorters, do all steps of Wisdom Thinking, but they love being given chances to make choices. Let your child choose and succeed. Let your child choose and fail. She will learn from both experiences.

School and relationships are the main activities. If you're a parent of a chooser, you'll need to help your child apply Wisdom Thinking to learning at school and learning away from school. During these years your child will have choices about which classes she takes. If she is planning to go on to college, discuss which courses will be most beneficial, and why. Thinking about the future is a big part of preparing for adulthood. College and job plans are important choices that need the skills of a Wisdom Thinker.

In addition to school, there is a diversion which takes up hours of thinking time. Relationships grab the spotlight. Talk with your child about lasting friendships, work relationships, and romantic involvements. Learning how to think about others is central to your child's ability to make wise choices for herself and those around her.

INDIVIDUAL DIFFERENCES

You've now met the Average Children: Gertie Gatherer, Sam Sorter, and Chelsea Chooser.

Somewhere in those descriptions you have probably recognized a little bit of your own child. But maybe some of the activities mentioned would not interest him, or perhaps he is in a category that doesn't correspond with his age. Don't worry. You can still teach him Wisdom Thinking. But you'll need to make some minor adjustments to tailor your teaching to meet his needs.

The Advanced or Delayed Child

If your child is becoming a sorter while his peers are still gatherers, that is normal for him. He is probably a little advanced. Or if he's a sorter while his peers are choosers, that is fine too. His development is a little slower. Both advanced and delayed children are able to learn to think.

The important key to remember in dealing with exceptions to the rule is *give these children room to be different.* Allow them to develop at their own pace. Trying to move your child on when he isn't ready will not work. Skills that need to be learned will go undeveloped. In addition, it will be discouraging for him to feel like he must scramble to keep up.

Holding children back is also unwise. If your child is advanced, try to keep up with his changing interests. Children who are ready to move ahead, but are not allowed to, often become bored. They lose interest in what is being taught, and sometimes cause mischief.

Wherever your child is developmentally, let him grow as he will. Wisdom Thinking can still be taught. Let him be a kid, but let him be a wise kid.

Personality Differences

Maybe your child is right in the ball park as far as development for her age is concerned, yet she doesn't seem to think the way you would expect. Perhaps you can't get her to sit still long enough to rub two thoughts together. Or maybe she sits silently for so long that you think she's fallen asleep. These kinds of differences can be the result of personality.

The two major categories of personality are the reflective type and the impulsive type. Reflective children usually prefer quieter activities, and often like to read. They feel most at ease with one or two friends at a time. They enjoy ideas and thinking, and may spend hours alone with their thoughts. Though slow to get started, their plans are often well thought-out.

Impulsive children, on the other hand, enjoy being active. They want to be doing rather than thinking. As a result, they may get a lot done but make many mistakes. You can always tell where they've been by the messy trail they leave behind them.

Both personality types usually soften as years go by. The reflective child will get more done as she is forced to deal with the world outside her thoughts. The impulsive child will change too as she experiences the negative results of her impulsive choices.

When teaching thinking to these two types of children, you may find your impulsive child resisting your suggestion to think before acting. But she needs to develop Wisdom Thinking skills to make the most of her activity. The reflective child may need help putting thought into action. She may need a push to put those good ideas to work. Whatever her personality, she needs to learn to be a wise thinker. Reflective or impulsive, young or old, all children can become Wisdom Thinkers.

YOU TRY IT!
(BY GETTING TO KNOW THESE KIDS)

Now take some time to get to know real growing children like Gertie, Sam, and Chelsea. Complete a worksheet for your child. Or better yet, complete a worksheet for three children. If you don't have a Gertie, Sam, or Chelsea of your own, borrow a child you know in that age group. Why not have breakfast with a *Gatherer* (ages three, four, or five). Do lunch with a *Sorter* (ages six to twelve). And dine out with a *Chooser* (ages thirteen to eighteen). Filling out a worksheet for each of the age groups will help you see the differences in the way they think.

HAVE BREAKFAST WITH A GATHERER
(THREE TO FIVE YEARS OLD)

Plan Ahead

Who are you meeting?
What is his or her age?
When will you meet together?
Where will you meet?

Listen

What is your favorite thing to do?
Where is your favorite place to go?
What is your favorite food to eat?
Do you have any brothers or sisters? What do you like to do with your brother? What do you like to do with your sister?

Do you have any pets? What kind? What are their names? How do you take care of them? What do you like to do with them?

What do you like to do inside your house? (You may need to ask, "What do you like to play inside your house?")

What do you like to do outside?

If you were going to build a tree fort, would you draw plans first or get wood, nails, and a hammer and start building?

If you had ten dollars to spend, would you sit down and take time to plan how you would spend it, or would you want to go right to the store and look at things to buy?

What is friendship?

Do Lunch with a Sorter
(Six to Twelve Years Old)

Plan Ahead

Who are you meeting?

What is his or her age?

When will you meet together?

Where will you meet?

Listen

What is your favorite thing to do?

Where is your favorite place to go?

What is your favorite food to eat?

Do you like to read? What do you usually read?

What is your favorite school subject? Why?

What do you do when you get home from school?

Do you have any jobs at your house? What are they?

Would you rather paint pictures of nature or race cars?

If someone gave you twenty-five dollars what would you do with it?

What is friendship?

DINE OUT WITH A CHOOSER
(THIRTEEN TO EIGHTEEN YEARS OLD)

Plan Ahead

Who are you meeting?

What is his or her age?

When will you meet together?

Where will you meet?

Listen

What is your favorite thing to do?

Where is your favorite place to go?

What is your favorite food to eat?

What do you like most about school? What do you like least about school?

What careers interest you most?

When you are not in school, what are you usually doing?

What's a normal day like for you? Walk me through from waking to sleeping.

Would you rather work with ideas and imagination or do activities?

What clothes would you wear if you could get anything you wanted? Go head to toe. Tell me about hats to shoes.

What is friendship?

CHAPTER SIX

Encouraging
Wisdom Thinking

Ellen's life seems like an endless track race from the moment she wakes up in the morning until she goes to bed at night. Divorced three years ago, she is the sole provider for herself and her two grade-school-aged children. When she thinks about how she's raising her kids, she often feels like a failure. It seems there aren't enough hours in the day to do all the things she would like to do with them.

Ellen tries to set aside time with each child after dinner in the evening. But sometimes the tiredness washes over her like a powerful wave, and she nods off in the chair while the kids watch TV. That makes her feel guilty. And she fears they look more often to each other or the baby-sitter than to her for advice about their school problems.

Ellen wants to teach her children to make wise choices about their lives. But she isn't sure how to help them, especially with her limited time and resources. Ellen isn't the only one who feels this way. Life today is busy for all kinds of families. I imagine all of us feel overwhelmed and inadequate at times. I sure do. But to teach Wisdom Thinking, we don't have to be super-mom or super-dad. Much of Wisdom Thinking is conveyed in the way we accomplish simple day-to-day tasks. And as our children observe the way we think, they'll learn just from watching us.

BE A WISDOM-THINKING PARENT

A child who learns to think at home has parents who value good thinking. Just as Timothy in the New Testament learned the life of faith from his mother, Eunice, and his grandmother, Lois (2 Timothy 1:5), children learn to think by watching their parents. One of the most important things you can do to mold your child into a Wisdom Thinker is to make your home an environment where wise thinking takes place. You can do this in two ways. First, by practicing Wisdom Thinking in front of your child. Second, by actively teaching your child to think with wisdom.

Perhaps you're saying, "Whoa! That sounds like too much. I'm like Ellen. I don't have any more hours in the day." Great, that's fine. Wisdom Thinking doesn't have to add to your busy schedule. You can teach Wisdom Thinking under any and all circumstances.

I've found that teaching thinking mostly involves a change in my own mental attitude. Now that I know more about the thinking skills I want to teach to my children, I can spot teaching opportunities as they arise. It might be while we're doing family chores or when we're going out to eat or when I'm talking with Sarah or Josh on a walk or a bike-ride. A simple word of encouragement or small suggestion is sometimes all I do to help them focus on their thinking and choices. Sometimes that's all that's needed. And every little bit helps.

As you're reading this chapter, think about little ways you can encourage wise thinking as you go about your daily routine. But don't make any big plans to change your lifestyle. You don't have to.

BEING A GOOD EXAMPLE

Being an example is easy. Being a good example is not. It takes some effort to be a living, breathing, how-to manual on Wisdom Thinking. But the effort is worth it when our children show they are learning how to think. We all need to consider the example we are to our children. The following questions will help you evaluate the example you convey to your child:

Do I let my child see me solving problems? Do I approach problems with a positive attitude? Or do I resent problems? Do I believe God will guide my thinking? Do I look forward to thinking because I know it is rewarding?

Do I practice gathering, sorting, and choosing? Do I think about my thinking?

Do I consult the Word for help? Ask wise counselors? Pray before choosing? In front of my child, do I ever discuss how I thought through an issue and why I came to my conclusion?

None of us can give positive answers to these questions all the time. But we must remember that our children do not see only what we want them to see. They see what we do. They need to see Wisdom Thinking in our actions.

BEING A THINKING TEACHER

I have a friend who is a wonderful teacher. In her classroom, even "dull" subjects are made fun and exciting because she relates them to real-life situations. If there is an excited circle of students in one corner of the room, you'll find her at the center guiding, directing, and sharing their discovery. Her sense of excitement and love of learning motivates her students. They become learners themselves. She learns along with them. And that, too, is part of good teaching.

My friend is an excellent example for parents who want to teach their children to think. Kids learn better when they are taught by someone who is enthusiastic about learning. And educators are now placing more emphasis on the importance of teaching skills using real-life situations. This is great news for parents who have been teaching this way since Adam and Eve warned Cain and Abel to watch out for snakes while picking fruit for dinner. Keep teaching using real-life situations, but teach with a purpose. Teach thinking.

Look for natural opportunities to teach thinking in everyday experiences. Teach thinking as you discuss events from school. What does your child gather from the behavior of others? When an argument with friends is in progress, what does he plan to do?

Watch television programs together and discuss what he gathered. Sort out the behavior of the characters. Would he make the same choices? Read the books your child reads, including school textbooks. Help him evaluate what he is learning. Does your child have a special area of interest? Jump on that area and teach him to gather, sort, and choose.

Take a close look at how your child thinks right now. Throw away expectations which say he must be like every other child. Cory was overly-dependent on others to make decisions for her. Though she was in high school, her mother still picked out her clothes for school each morning. Of course, Cory's mom had contributed to this problem. But when she realized Cory would be on her own at college in just a year, she began pressing Cory to make her own choices. Cory did so reluctantly at first. It was only after several months and a few compliments from friends that she became confident about her clothing choices. Eventually she began to enjoy putting her own outfits together, which led to shopping trips to buy more clothes, which led to more choices. But it was an important step for Cory.

It's never too late to start working on weaknesses or reinforcing strengths. Why not stop right now and think about how your child thinks. Is there an area of weakness you can identify? Is he impulsive? Irresponsible? Uninformed about God's Word? What about strengths? Can you comment positively on some aspect of his choice-making? Now that you're familiar with the three skills of Wisdom Thinking and your child's age-related abilities, pick an area of weakness you can help to strengthen. Think about a strength you want to reinforce. What would you like to work on this week, this month, this year? This will help you get started and keep you on the right track.

Parents are in the best position to teach their children. Most know their "student" better than any paid educator. We have no workbook we have to finish this year, no grades we have to calculate, and no limitation on what we can discuss and discover with our children. Enjoy watching your child grow as you emphasize thinking during your time together.

PROVIDE A RICH ENVIRONMENT

In order to make wise decisions, your thinker needs information. And she needs experience using it.

Use Those Good Senses

Your child takes in information through her senses. And seeing the world through a child's eyes can be great fun for parents. Look at the beauty of the universe, and the not-so-beautiful, together. Listen to the many sounds that enrich our lives, voices that speak of joy, hope, and pain. Touch and handle God's creation and feel a sense of wonder together. Taste the flavors of the world and smell the aromas. Enjoy using your senses together to understand the people and places you visit.

Asking "Why?"

Teach your child to be a "why person." Asking why is a good way to gain knowledge. When I was in college a girl in one of my classes always had to ask, "Why?" Each day, as the rest of us groaned and rolled our eyes, the professor would patiently answer her oft-repeated question. One day after several weeks of class the girl was absent. The professor took some time that day to explain why he loved it when people ask why. He told us to think about how much we had learned from her constant questioning. He suspected she had asked why when others in the class were afraid to. And he was right. Her "why" questions enhanced our class and helped all of us to learn.

Gatherers naturally go through a "why stage." But as any parent knows, it can be irritating to constantly hear that three-letter word.

"Mommy, why does my teacher give me homework?"

"Because she wants to be sure you learn your math well."

"Why?"

"Because math is an important part of what we do everyday."

"Why?"

"Because the world is made up of things to count, and add, and subtract."

"Why?"

"Stop saying 'why'—I don't know!"

Maybe we don't like the question "why?" because we're afraid of saying, "I don't know." Whatever the reason, asking why is a trait we often don't like in children but often admire in adults. Let your child continue to ask you, "Why?" And use those opportunities to teach thinking.

Provide Information for Your Child

Another way to encourage thinking is to give your child access to information she could not otherwise obtain by herself. This doesn't have to cost a lot of money. Remember the library is there for your use. Check out books and magazines. Purchase an atlas, a dictionary, and an encyclopedia. The money will be well-spent. Watch television and rent movies. Discuss together what you see, hear, and feel. Visiting friends and relatives will add new viewpoints to her life. Go to cultural events, observe government in action, plan trips to historical sites. Help her develop a strong base of "inside" information.

Kids love it when we help them investigate interests while their curiosity is at its peak. Let's face it, force-feeding doesn't work with most children. But when your child wants to know why there are twenty-four hours in a day or what life is like in Yugoslavia, this is the time to also teach thinking. Maybe you have the books at home to answer those questions. Or go to the library and gather information about the earth's rotation. Pick up the "XYZ" volume of the encyclopedia and read about Yugoslavia. Moving quickly to investigate interests will not only answer her questions, it will teach her how to think and solve her own problems.

TEACH YOUR CHILD HOW TO THINK WITH OTHERS

Do you remember what it was like to work on a group project at school? In your corner of the room, one kid sat on the fringes looking bored. He never said anything. Next to him, the cut-up squirmed around trying his best to avoid being serious. A couple of girls spent the entire time giggling and whispering about their boyfriends. The rest talked about the assignment. Out of this little knot emerged the leader who told everybody what to do.

Were you ever happy with your group's results? If you were the uncompromising dictator, you probably were. If you were any of the others, you don't have such fond memories. Do groups always have to be this way? *No!*

Children who are taught to think cooperatively can make groups into productive units. One year in library class I asked the eighth graders to participate in a poster-making contest to promote library use. I grouped the class into three- to four-person "advertising agencies." Each had to come up with a slogan and design. Next they chose jobs for each member of the group—who would draw, color, letter, and so on. When the posters were finished the class judged them.

After watching the groups work together, it was no surprise to me who won. It wasn't the group with the best artist or the most "brains." The winner was a group who started cooperating with each other from the moment they sat down. Working together, they accomplished more in a shorter time than any of the rest. And their work was voted best by their peers.

What a Good Group Member Knows

Valuing the thinking of others is central to good group work. When others suggest a solution to a problem, we need to show them that we appreciate those ideas and insights. My children love to hear that I like their ideas too. When we act on our children's suggestions they feel like a valued group member.

Pooled experience is helpful and should be used. People can come up with better ideas when they work together and share from a large pool of experience than they can on their own. One idea can lead to another until all have contributed to the best idea of all.

Competition keeps groups from thinking well together. In our society, we too often teach competition rather than cooperation. We teach it in our families too. In our struggle to be the best, we sometimes jealously guard our ideas from others. We want to be the one person who thinks of the most clever idea and saves the day. But when we fail to share knowledge, we end up making choices based on limited information.

Working in a group can be fun and productive. Committees have gotten a bad name over the years, and part of the reason is probably the competition factor. But fun groups are often some of the most creative and productive groups around. Laughing helps us relax. When we relax, we tend to think better. A silly idea can be the start of a great solution. Good group members aren't afraid to have fun.

Wise thinkers know that more information leads to more complete thinking. Thinking together, a group will be better than any of its members would be alone.

Pass On Healthy Attitudes about Thinking

Good attitudes foster good thinking. So it is

important for your child to learn a proper concept of what thinking is. Remember:

Thinking is a skill; wise thinkers are made, not born. Believing thinking is a skill will encourage your child to work at developing it. This attitude also helps us to be patient when our child makes mistakes, for we know we are all in the life-long process of learning to be wise.

Thinking is to be valued, for it leads us on to thinking and acting rightly. Being thoughtful isn't just for eggheads with pocket-protectors and slide rules. Everyone benefits from taking time to think. But our culture has long admired "dumb blonds" and "thick-headed athletes." Fight against those stereotypes with your child. Teach her to value thinking.

Thinking is fun and rewarding; it feels good to do your best and to experience a wise result. Discard those images of frowning thinkers who are always grumpy and have no time for play. Most people who think for a living do it because they enjoy it. Solving problems is like doing puzzles. Each piece that fits brings a sense of satisfaction. The final picture is evidence of being able to make hundreds of little jagged edges match perfectly. Fitting the pieces together in real life brings greater joy and thankfulness to God.

BE SURE THE HEART IS IN YOUR WISDOM-THINKING HOME

The heart of Wisdom Thinking is Thinking about God. To think and act wisely, children must be well-acquainted with God and his Word. We are responsible to introduce our children to their Maker and encourage them to include Bible reading, wise counsel, and prayer in all kinds of thinking.

It is tempting to leave all that "church stuff" up to the pastor or Sunday school teacher. But biblical instruction one day of each week isn't enough for anyone. Wisdom Thinking must be practiced every day. Little decisions count, and your child needs you to help her see how Bible commands and principles affect her day-to-day choices.

Zack's best friend, Logan, was a classic manipulator. He used unkind words and criticism to "put down" anyone he wished to control. Zack's parents were concerned about Logan's worldly influence on their son and often restricted the amount of time they spent together. Zack couldn't see the problem. In fact, he became angry with his parents for not allowing him the freedom to play with Logan whenever he wanted to.

Zack was a growing Christian, however, and his family read and discussed the Bible together regularly. Occasionally Zack would point out things about Logan that were definitely not pleasing to God. But it made little difference in his desire to spend time with his friend.

A turning point came when others outside the family noticed Zack had picked up some manipulating habits himself. He began using criticism to control others and to elevate his own self-image. When a friend pointed this out, Zack remembered some of the things Logan had said to him. He realized these attitudes were the very ones he had recognized as not being pleasing to God.

Zack talked to his mom about his problem. He decided he had better not spend so much time with Logan. He also began to see Logan more clearly and didn't admire him so much. But he was still drawn to him, and as he grew up it was a continuing struggle to not be overly influenced by Logan.

We need to make our homes places where our children, like Zack, learn to think about God. Let's talk about God with our children. We can show them how mature thinkers include him in their thinking. And together our families can learn to make thinking truly wise.

You Try It!

Now take some time to think about the places your child spends most of her time. What does she like to do most in those places? Answering the following questions will help you see how you can fit Wisdom Thinking training into your normal daily routine. Use your own observations and ask your son or daughter for input.

1. Number the places listed below from one to eight. Label the place your child spends the most time as number one; label the place your child spends the least time as number eight.

___ own room

___ house

___ neighborhood

___ school

___ church

___ day care or baby-sitter's house

___ relative's house

___ friend's house

2. Now, circle three of the places you are most often present with your child.

3. Next, describe each of these places:

Place One

List five things your child is most likely to use in this place. Toys? Books and magazines? Electronic devices? Bicycles and skateboards? Dolls? Baseball bats?

_____

_____

_____

_____

List five activities your child is most likely to do in this place. Read? Watch TV? Pretend? Play board games or athletic games?

_____

_____

_____

_____

Place Two

List five things your child is most likely to use in this place. Toys? Books and magazines? Electronic devices? Bicycles and skateboards? Dolls? Baseball bats?

_____

_____

_____

_____

List five activities your child is most likely to do in this place. Read? Watch TV? Pretend? Play board games or athletic games?

_____

_____

_____

_____

Place Three

List five things your child is most likely to use in this place. Toys? Books and magazines? Electronic devices? Bicycles and skateboards? Dolls? Baseball bats?

_____

_____

_____

_____

List five activities your child is most likely to do in this place. Read? Watch TV? Pretend? Play board games or athletic games?

_____

_____

_____

_____

Now read on to find out how you can incorporate Wisdom Thinking practice into the activities in these places.

CHAPTER SEVEN

Practice Makes Wise Thinkers

Piano lessons—what child can escape them? I didn't. Most weeks I practiced faithfully, but I have to admit, some weeks I did not. When I didn't practice, no matter how hard I tried, I couldn't pull the wool over my teacher's ears. She could always tell when I had spent the past few days pretending the piano did not exist. Not only did I not improve, my playing actually got worse. My fingers became stiff and uncooperative.

Thinking skills are much the same. When we don't use thinking skills regularly, they're not automatic. After a while, we may forget them. So kids who are just learning how to think need plenty of practice using their new skills. Make thinking practice part of your daily home life and give your child plenty of chances to test and refine her Wisdom Thinking.

MAKE WISDOM THINKING PART OF YOUR CHILD'S LIFE

Wisdom Thinking is easily added to your family's routine. Remember, it doesn't require changing your schedule. You don't have to add a certain number of hours every week to practice. You don't need to set aside extra teaching time because Wisdom Thinking is best taught through real-life, day-to-day situations. Noel and I are going to offer many suggestions in this chapter about how you can fit thinking practice into your family life. Some of these suggestions may be workable for your family, others may seem impractical. Gather, sort, and choose to determine what is useful for you and what isn't. Every little bit you do will help your child, but don't feel you have to do everything we suggest.

Make Wisdom Thinking part of your daily routine. If you and your child are "morning people" you can start Wisdom Thinking bright and early. Gather by talking about what goes into a well-balanced breakfast. What are the four food groups? Move on to sorting. What do we have in the house to eat today? Give her the chance to choose. What nutritional foods would she pick to eat? If you pack a lunch for school, have her help with that too. Then let her demonstrate her thinking skills by taking responsibility for the books, homework, and lunch that must be stowed in her backpack. This too is part of learning to think. It involves planning ahead, choosing how to use her time wisely, and thinking independently.

Use the methods. When your child is home from school you can continue with the same type of casual teaching you did at breakfast time. Or you could use one of the methods in the third section of this book for a little special time together. Playful Thinking and Storytelling will show you how to have fun learning to think together. Controlled Experience tells how to set up thinking opportunities for your child. Rethinking will help you follow up his choices by talking afterward. Bible Search and Research will help you apply Bible knowledge to thinking and choices. Media Critique will teach you how to help him evaluate what he reads, sees, and hears.

Think together. Children can pick up thinking skills by being involved in family discussions. The Morrison family has weekly meetings to talk over problems, plan upcoming events, and share ideas. During this time, everyone contributes to discussions. This involves thinking together as a group and reinforces those group skills you learned about in the last chapter. Family pow-wows are also good opportunities for parents to think in front of their child. And it gives moms and dads a chance to explain why they make certain decisions.

Ask others to help. Sometimes it's helpful to let others know what your goals are for teaching thinking to your child. Who can you tell? Grandma and Grandpa, your next door neighbor, some of your close family friends. Maybe they will be willing to help accomplish your goals. They might be willing to teach thinking skills as part of their time with your child. My mother took Sarah clothes shopping for her tenth birthday. The two of them had a great time going from store to store. Together they compared styles, prices, and quality. When Sarah came home, she was totally satisfied with her purchases. Nana was satisfied too. I was excited because my mom turned a little birthday fling into a teaching opportunity they both enjoyed.

Teach thinking through activities. Thinking can be taught when planning family activities. Vacation travels, events in your city, trips to the zoo, and visits with friends can all be fertile ground for gathering, sorting, and choosing. Planning an outing is thinking ahead. Where will you go? What will you do? Why are you doing this? While you are engaged in your activity, gather information, sort options, and choose together. Afterward, discuss your choices. Think about what happened. What did you learn? Rejoice in the good; learn together how to avoid the bad.

Real-life situations are the best way for children to learn and understand. And you don't have to take away precious hours from other activities to teach thinking. Look at common daily events as avenues to Wisdom Thinking. It is surprising how many times each day you can find teaching moments. Activities that once were routine become new and different when you see how they can be used for thinking training. Remember, the more your child practices, the better thinker she becomes. The better thinker she becomes, the better choices she'll make.

BUILD ON SUCCESS

Learning Wisdom Thinking is a step-by-step process. It would be nice if children could use the skills perfectly after a short seminar, but it doesn't work that way. Even adults don't learn new skills like that. *Wisdom* in Proverbs is the same Hebrew word used to describe the trained, skilled (wise) hands of Hebrew craftsmen. These craftsmen spent years as apprentices observing the masters and testing their skills until they, too, mastered their craft. In the same way, we become skilled, wise thinkers through practice. And thinking skill practice involves starting with simple tasks. Then, when that task is mastered, thinkers move on to more difficult challenges. This is building on success.

Use common events to test wise thinking. Most privileges or tasks can be used to test thinking skills. Let your child try to do his own thinking to see how well he can do. When your child has passed a thinking test, build on success. Bonnie's children, ages six and eight, were never allowed to cross the street alone. Bonnie always went with them. She told them when it was safe to cross and then watched until they were safely on the other side. Bonnie felt this was the only way to ensure their safety.

Then one day Bonnie watched her neighbor, Candy, at the curb with her five-year-old, Christy. Candy said, "Christy, you tell me when you know it's safe to cross the street." Christy looked both ways, then said, "No cars are coming. It's safe now." Candy agreed. Candy and Christy did this every day for several weeks until Candy was satisfied that Christy could make the decision herself. Bonnie decided Candy had the right idea. Following Candy's method, Bonnie's children were soon able to demonstrate that they, too, could cross safely alone.

You can use this same method to build on success throughout your child's growing years. Preteens can work up to baby-sitting brothers and sisters; teens can work their way up to borrowing the car. The key is to start with simple thinking and easy choices. Then as your child shows he can think wisely, increase the difficulty and the responsibility.

Managing money is a common activity parents use to teach thinking. Jim began by giving his son Kyle fifty cents a week when Kyle was four. Kyle kept two envelopes in his room. One envelope was for his church offering, the other for his savings. Each week he would put some of his money in each envelope. Every other week, Kyle would take his church money to Sunday school and give it as an offering.

As Kyle grew older he showed he could resist spending all of his allowance the minute he got it. Jim then gave him a dollar per week. Following the same envelope procedure, Kyle proved again he was responsible with his money. Jim raised his allowance and also added to his responsibilities. New envelopes were added for clothing and school supplies which Kyle budgeted out of his adequate allowance.

When Kyle was in high school, he got his first part-time job. Shortly after he began working, Jim and Kyle decided to go to a baseball game. But Jim was short of cash so he asked Kyle for a loan. Kyle replied, "Dad, you should really learn how to budget your money a little better."

Kyle was able to move smoothly from one success to another. This isn't unheard of, but most often failure is also part of learning to think.

DEALING WITH FAILURE

Observing a growing Wisdom Thinker is like watching the incoming tide of the ocean. With every breaker the water inches further onto the sand. But before each new wave arrives, the water pulls back, seemingly in defeat. Then it crashes in even further up the beach. The tide reaches its highest point only after many attempts. Learning to think is a tidal dance of two steps forward, one step back, but those steps back can be used to learn how to move ahead. Failure is an important part of learning to think.

Free to fail. We must give our children the freedom to fail, which means we must allow our kids to make real choices that have real consequences. I don't mean you should set your child up for a fall. But on the other hand, do not program success into all of her choices. Through failure she will learn firsthand just how bad "bad choices" can be.

It is natural for parents to want to protect their children as much as possible from evil and danger. And that is certainly part of our responsibility. Preschoolers need us to tell them when it is safe to go across the street. Teens need supervision on the street when they are learning to drive. But at some point your child will demonstrate her skills in your presence, and then you will know it is time for her to try making those crucial choices on her own. And you should let her.

Allow consequences. Along with the freedom to fail, your child needs to experience the consequences of his choices. That, too, is difficult to watch. Seeing my children in *f* pain, whether emotional or physical, is a wrenching experience. But often they made a choice that led to that pain. I can comfort them and show care and concern, but it isn't helpful to let them choose unwisely and then shield them from the result of their choice.

Ten-year-old Simon did not get along with Paul and Nat. He was jealous of their friendship. He felt left out. So he made up a story about Nat and Paul cheating on a math test. Paul and Nat were confronted by their teacher, but they denied any wrongdoing. They offered to take another test as proof of their sincerity. The teacher, aware of Simon's jealously, asked if he made the story up. He admitted he did.

Simon's parents were told of his escapade, but they didn't want their son punished. They felt he had made up the story because he was hurt, and they felt sorry for him. Simon's parents never asked him to apologize to the boys he had falsely accused. And Simon? He continued to harass Nat and Paul for the rest of the year.

Failure without consequences does not teach Wisdom Thinking. It teaches the exact opposite. It creates children who are ill-prepared to function in our very real world.

Recovery from failure. Since failure is so important, wise thinkers must learn how to recover from poor choices. What do they do? They admit they made a mistake and they accept the consequences. They figure out where their thinking failed and they try to avoid making the same mistake in the future.

Again, the best way to teach your child to admit his mistakes and accept the consequences is to admit your own mistakes and accept the consequences. Many of us find it difficult to admit our failures to each other. It's harder still to admit our failures to our children. But when we show our children that mistakes are part of our own lives, they will be more likely to admit it when they make mistakes. Rationalizing mistakes, blaming them on someone else, or blaming them on some circumstance hinders learning how to make a better choice next time.

It is helpful to go over choices with your child to discover where thinking went wrong. Did he gather enough information to make a wise choice? Or did he just do what "felt right"? Did he follow biblical commands? Was he given good advice which he rejected? If you can pinpoint the problem, it will not only teach him to make a better choice next time, but it will also teach him how to be a better thinker.

After a bad experience, it is important to let your child try again. This is the only way you can find out if she has learned from her mistakes. If she makes another thinking mistake, the process must be repeated until the skill is mastered. But once it is mastered, remember to move on to greater thinking difficulty so that your child can continue to grow in wisdom.

Say Rah-Rah for Wisdom Thinkers

Josh went to soccer camp last summer. On the last day, families were invited to watch a mini-game. Many of us milled around, quietly clenching our teeth while our sons crashed and bashed on the field. But one mom, Mrs. Estep, participated more than the rest of us. She yelled during the whole match. And she didn't just yell for her son. She called out encouragement to kids on both teams. As the match wore on and the boys ran out of gas, Mrs. Estep yelled louder. No kick or block escaped her notice. Now and then one of the boys would look over and grin at their one-person rally squad, obviously delighted at her enthusiasm.

Mrs. Estep was doing a great job being a supportive crowd all by herself. And it was a good thing, because the rest of us were only letting out embarrassed and anemic "Yeahs!" now and again. Finally Sarah asked me, "Mom, why aren't you yelling for Josh like Mrs. Estep?"

We need to encourage our young thinkers like I needed to encourage Josh at soccer. Kids need to know when they are doing a good job. Encouragement provides the incentive they need to keep trying. Praise makes them want to do the right thing again and again. But it's often easiest for parents to speak up only when their child makes a thinking error.

We shouldn't be surprised when our children act like immature thinkers. They are. But along with gently correcting them, we must try to find something good to say about the part of thinking they did well. Even if your child didn't make the right choice, maybe he did a good job gathering and sorting options. Or maybe he made a wrong choice, but for a good reason. Praise him for his good thinking.

Sometimes, rewarding your child for good thinking is easier said than done. Often it is difficult to see improvement. Noel is an expert at finding good things to say to students. One day he asked his students to write a half-page summary on a book they had been reading. One boy struggled the whole time. After ten minutes, his paper was smudged and torn from numerous erasings. Noel tried to read the two sentences he had written, but they were indecipherable. He asked the student to read them out loud. But he couldn't read them either. So Noel said, "Well, I think you're going to have to do this over. But I *did* notice you gripped your pencil correctly today."

Thinking growth is sometimes hidden. Like a butterfly forming in its chrysalis, your child may be doing some wonderful maturing without your knowledge. You can't see it happening. Therefore, you must look carefully for evidence of growth in the choices he makes.

Big successes result from learning through little steps. So, when your child thinks wisely about little things—such as choosing to do homework over watching television, or putting water out for the dog on a hot day instead of ignoring his needs—tell him he did well. Your words of encouragement can be the incentive to transfer the skill he practiced to bigger choices. Your child needs to hear the words, "That was wise thinking!"

Praise from you is essential because good choices your child makes may be ridiculed by friends. Stacy, a high school senior, was trying to make wise choices. Engaged to Tom, a sophomore in college, she looked forward to her August wedding. That is, until one of her "friends" began taunting her about her lack of sexual experience. Stacy had decided to remain a virgin until marriage, but the ridicule from her friend filled the last few months of single life with doubt about her choice and anxiety about her future.

When our children choose not to imitate peers, not to swear, smoke, gossip, cheat, or steal, few of their friends are likely to applaud them. Good choices sometimes make people unpopular. And promise of future reward in heaven may seem meaningless when our sons and daughters are faced with harassment today.

So be your thinker's number-one supporter. Cheer him on in his efforts to make wise choices. Give him the incentive to keep trying. After all, Wisdom Thinking is worth cheering about.

PRACTICE WITH THE METHODS

Up until now, Noel and I have talked about making Wisdom Thinking a part of your daily routine. But you can focus even more on wise thinking by using some of the suggested methods explained in the next section. You can pick and choose which of these methods you'd like to use. Your choice depends on your family's interests and the ages of your children. Each chapter explains a method then ends with a worksheet designed to help you plan how you will do a thinking activity. So you'll have some idea of what the methods are about, I've summarized them below. Have fun trying out those you like best with your whole family.

Chapter 8: Playful Thinking. Playful Thinking activities teach thinking through fun family involvement. They work because they are fun and lighthearted. Though they are more structured than the free-for-all play that children often engage in, they can be just as enjoyable. Playful Thinking activities are: Playacting, Role-Playing, Role-Switching, Simulation, and Thinking Games.

Chapter 9: Storytelling. Nothing captures the mind of a child like a good story. We are all familiar with folk and fairy tales passed from one person to another, from generation to generation. But two other kinds of storytelling are common as well: oral history and the reading of storybooks. All three can be used to teach thinking.

Chapter 10: Controlled Experience. A controlled experience is any situation where your child can practice Wisdom Thinking under supervision. Your child is allowed to test her thinking skill. She makes choices, but you watch the whole process. If she needs your help, you are there to give it.

Chapter 11: Rethinking. Rethinking is talking about your child's thinking after he has tested his skills. It can follow a good or bad, planned or unplanned event. By rethinking, you can evaluate how well or poorly he formed opinions or made decisions. You can use it to decide if your child should be rewarded for good thinking or if correction is needed.

Chapter 12: Bible Search and Research. Help your child learn to answer his own questions. Bible Search and Research Skills will teach him how to gather outside information. He will learn how to do a Bible search, and how to gather information outside the Bible.

Chapter 13: Media Critique. Mass media is a fixture of American life. When radio alarms go off in the morning, media says: "Good morning, America." Media in its various forms sits on coffee tables across the nation. Children need to learn how to gather, sort, and choose from print, film, and music.

YOU TRY IT!

It's time to give your growing thinker some practice. Take what you learned from the activities following chapters 5 and 6 and plan how to include Wisdom Thinking into daily activities.

With whom will you practice? Is she a gatherer, a sorter, or a chooser?

Choose a place you described in You Try It! from chapter 6 for this activity.

When will you do it?

What thinking activity will you use in that place? Look in the previous section for a description of the thinking activities listed below:

8. Playful Thinking

9. Storytelling

10. Controlled Experiences

11. Rethinking

12. Bible Search and Research

13. Media Critique

Putting It All Together

Two row houses stand side by side on a quiet street. The houses look identical. They were designed by the same architect, built by the same builder, and landscaped by the same contractor. The families that live in these homes are similar too. Each has a father, mother, and three children. Both dads have good jobs. The moms work part-time. The kids attend good schools.

To find any differences in the two houses, you have to look inside. The Wilsons' house is decorated with expensive furnishings. It is kept immaculately. The Bartons' home, on the other hand, is rather messy. The furniture is older, the carpet a bit worn.

The Wilsons and the Bartons, who seem so similar on the outside, are different on the inside. Let's spend some time in each of their homes on a typical Sunday afternoon. It's the one time of the week when all members of both families are sure to be home.

The Wilsons

Cliff and Yvonne Wilson look forward to Sunday. It's the one day of the week when they don't have to go anywhere if they don't want to. So they usually sleep in until at least 11:00. The children, Troy (15), Vicki (11), and Joy (6), make their own breakfast and watch TV until their parents get up. If the weather is good, they sometimes go out and play with friends.

By the time noon rolls around, Cliff can be found watching sports on TV. Yvonne is rushing around the house, picking up after the family. It seems there aren't enough hours in the week for her to keep the house as nice as she would like. Sometimes she gets after the kids to clean their own rooms, but more often she does it alone. It's just easier to do it herself.

It seems the Wilson kids bicker a lot on Sundays. If they take their fight to Cliff, he yells at them to quiet down so he can hear the game. Yvonne usually steps in to settle the fight. But she has so much to do on Sunday that she wishes the kids would solve their own problems. Joy is the worst distraction. She shadows Yvonne, asking questions about anything and everything. Yvonne tries to be patient, but ends up telling Joy to go outside and play and "Leave Mommy alone so she can get her work done."

Troy sometimes watches sports with Cliff. He used to ask questions about why the coaches choose certain plays. But Cliff would tell him, "It's too hard to explain." So Troy has learned not to ask anymore.

Vicki usually has homework to do, so she spends most of her Sunday afternoon trying to get it done. She gets stuck on some of her history questions now and then. Mom's typical answer to Vicki's requests for help is, "You know I hate history. And I'm too tired to think right now." So Vicki often asks Troy to help her out. This is risky since he isn't very patient. When he's in a bad mood, he tells her, "If you don't know the answer to that, you're really stupid." Vicki then has to wait to look up answers and definitions in the reference books at school. Going to the public library on the weekend is out of the question.

Sunday at the Wilsons ends with bathed children sitting in front of the TV watching a videotaped movie recommended by Troy's friend. Joy is scared by the violence, but Vicki comforts her. Dad snores lightly on the couch. Mom is still cleaning.

The Bartons

Ken and Jean Barton look forward to Sunday. It's the one time of the week the whole family is together all day. They start off the morning by going to church with their three children, Elise (13), Maggie (9), and Jeremy (5). After the service and Sunday school, the family has made it a tradition to go out to dinner. In the quiet of the restaurant, everyone has a chance to relax and talk about what they learned in church that morning. Though the meal is sometimes interrupted by Maggie and Jeremy kicking under the table, it is most often punctuated by laughter as the kids tell about the fun they had at Sunday school.

When they get home from eating out, they sometimes go for a hike in the woods or a visit with friends or relatives. If they stay home, Ken likes to watch sports like Cliff next door. Maggie has become interested in basketball because of the times she has watched it with her father. Together they've analyzed shooting styles of various players. Ken even put up a hoop out in the driveway where he and Maggie try to imitate famous players.

Jean does a little housework on Sunday like her neighbor Yvonne. Jeremy likes to "help" her. Jean doesn't get as much done with Jeremy around, and sometimes that frustrates her. His questions are never ending because he wants to know what Jean's doing. Jean realizes Jeremy won't always feel this way, so she takes time to teach him while he's curious.

Elise usually does her homework on Saturday so she can go to the library if necessary. But sometimes she leaves a little work for Sunday afternoon. She doesn't feel pressured because she knows her parents are willing to help her. She also has access to the family's reference library. It may be small, but it has the main books she needs to answer any general questions.

After a light Sunday dinner, the Bartons sit down together to watch a videotape on their VCR. Ken and Jean have previewed it, but they watch it with their children anyway. As the kids head off to bed, they are still talking about their favorite part of the movie. And they're all looking forward to their next Sunday together.

Which family is most likely to produce Wisdom-Thinking children?

Section Three

Methods for Teaching Wisdom Thinking

CHAPTER EIGHT

Playful Thinking

My husband, John, is really a kid at heart. So when he comes home from work, it's playtime. He teases Sarah and wrestles with Josh. But he also creates games that help our children learn to think.

John knows thinking is best taught through real-life situations. And for our children, play is still a large part of real life. When Sarah and Josh play with their dad, they often have no idea that he is teaching them thinking skills. Our house regularly resounds with giggles as John and the kids play one of their favorite games. The children run wildly through the house with the Daddy-monster in Frankenstein-like pursuit. Each time, Sarah or Josh must think up a new solution to thwart the monster. Sometimes all it takes to stop him is a kiss on the nose. Other times the kids team up to out-monster him, and scare their father into "tears." Because they're all having such a good time, it doesn't seem like learning to think at all. You can use play to teach Wisdom Thinking, too.

The following activities teach thinking through fun family involvement. Any of these activities will help teach thinking. Your family might want to try one or two or several of the ideas. But don't feel like you have to do them all. These are just suggestions. And feel free to modify them to fit your child's age, interests, and personality. To make these activities work, you'll want to keep them lighthearted. Though they are more structured than the free-for-all play that children often engage in, they are just as enjoyable. The following suggestions will get you started.

PLAYACTING
(CHILDREN AGES SIX TO TWELVE)

April and Noelle love to pretend. Hours speed swiftly by as they dress up like their mom, dad, movie stars, doctors, or ballerinas. Toy props become real in their active imaginations. They've become experts at acting out their own mini-dramas together. Both of them love to imagine what it would be like to be someone else.

Playacting uses this fascination with make-believe to teach thinking skills. The goal of playacting is to help your child practice Wisdom Thinking while acting out a part.

What You Will Need

When April and Noelle's mom decided to teach thinking through playacting, she sat down to think.

What would they need?

She decided to start with a little *story* for them all to act out. Mom thought fire safety would be a good theme. It was being emphasized in April's kindergarten class, and parents had been encouraged to talk to their children at home. They could act out what they would do if there was a fire in their house.

Other story ideas you might use emphasize relationships: student-teacher, child-parent, or child-friend. Health and nutrition ideas are always good. And character-building ideas like honesty and kindness fit well into playacting. Almost any idea that relates to real life, which your child can easily understand, will work.

Next, Mom thought about the parts the three of them would play. She decided to be the big sister. April and Noelle could choose their own names and be the little sisters. If you're going to try playacting, think of people your child knows: mom, dad, older or younger siblings, or grandparents. Friends and neighbors are fun parts to act: Mr. Thompson next door, the kids on the soccer team, or playmates down the street. Or choose to be workers in the community: firemen, doctors, dentists, bus drivers, policewomen, or shopkeepers. Many kids like to be the wise person who makes many of the decisions. And kids like it when their parent is the foolish person who must be told the right thing to do.

Last, Mom thought some *props* would come in handy. Both of her girls liked to dress up and Mom thought April and Noelle would feel and think more like their character if they were dressed for the part. To make the action seem real, Mom got out the fire extinguisher and a blanket for smothering flames. She prepared to push the button on the smoke alarm.

Other fun props to use are a toy doctor kit for a "visit to the doctor." Or if you're working on fire safety like April and Noelle's mom, the hose off your vacuum makes a great fire hose. If your play is about stealing, use a favorite family item that would be missed if it were stolen.

On with the Show

First, Mom talked about some basic fire-safety behavior (like touching a closed door to see if it's hot and staying close to the floor to avoid breathing smoke). Then she explained the fire story to April and Noelle. She said, "Let's pretend you're both in your rooms when there is a fire in the kitchen. The smoke alarm will go off. You both will need to escape as quickly as you can without going through the kitchen." After dressing up and renaming themselves, the girls began playing in their room as they normally would. Mom pressed the button on the smoke alarm and the action began.

If your play involves acting out an argument between friends, decide what happened to start the argument. If money has disappeared from Mom's purse, decide who took it and when it disappeared. Then let the play begin.

Mom kept the action moving by encouraging April and Noelle to act convincingly. At one point, they pretended April's clothes were on fire. April remembered to "stop—drop—and roll," the procedure she had learned at school. But Mom didn't interfere too much. She knew it would be more fun if the girls were allowed to act freely.

Review

When the fire-play was over, Mom and the girls discussed what happened. They talked about what was good thinking. April told about a bad choice she made. She had gone into the kitchen by mistake. She wouldn't make the same mistake next time.

If you or your child aren't satisfied with the outcome, you can act it out again. Or try switching parts and re-acting. Doing the play over again can help to reinforce good thinking.

ROLE-PLAYING
(ADOLESCENTS AGES THIRTEEN TO EIGHTEEN)

Grant was a little too old for playacting, but he enjoyed acting out parts too. In fact, he was trying out new roles in real life as he attempted to find out who he was and what his place was in society. Role-playing helped him find out more about other ways to think and act. While finding out about other options, he made some personal discoveries about himself.

The goal of role-playing is to help your child take on the role of an expert thinker. To do this, he will create his own script after researching his character. He can read about famous people in encyclopedias, history books, or biographies. As your child learns how his character thought and acted, he can then apply this type of behavior to a twentieth-century problem.

What You Will Need

Grant had been learning about racial prejudice in school. His father suggested they act out a situation where prejudice would be an issue. Grant thought he would pretend that a black family moved into their all-white neighborhood.

Other ideas to get your child to role-play are: Solve a crime in your own back yard, explore a "new frontier" in a forest, work on a science experiment together, or solve a personal dilemma.

Grant needed *characters* for his play. Since Abraham Lincoln had issued the Emancipation Proclamation, he would pretend he was Lincoln living today. He did some reading to find out how he might act. If your child likes science, find out about Newton, Einstein, or Pasteur. If he likes explorers, investigate Columbus, Lewis and Clark, or the Apollo astronauts. Who are his heroes of the faith? Have him investigate Abraham, David, Elijah, John the Baptist, or Paul. If he's working on a personal problem, have him learn about Christian counselors or pastors.

Grant didn't need many props since his was more of a philosophical discussion. But *props* are sometimes useful in acting out a role-play. If the role-play is about solving a crime, you'll need a crime scene complete with evidence. If you're being explorers, find a compass, mirror, knife, and other outdoor survival equipment. Props will help make your role-play more realistic.

On with the Role-play

Grant decided his parents would be the prejudiced neighbors fighting to keep the black family out of the neighborhood association. He took the role of the modern Abe Lincoln. They played their roles at a pretend meeting where Mom and Dad debated with "Abe" over granting the new black family membership in the association.

Role-playing works best if all roles are played out to their logical conclusion. And don't forget to inject consequences for poor thinking. If you're detectives like Sherlock Holmes and Dr. Watson, let Watson make some thinking errors that Holmes can point out. If you're Lewis and Clark exploring new frontiers, make some harmless judgment errors that your child can correct. Be a challenge to your thinker so he can exercise his thinking skills.

When the Curtain Comes Down

When Grant and his parents were done with their role-play, they reviewed thinking. Grant's parents were impressed by the number of good arguments "Abe" presented. But Grant learned that he needed some of "Abe's" diplomacy to not offend those listening.

When you are done with the role-play, ask some questions. Did your characters solve their problems? What went well? What went poorly? Did you enjoy thinking as your character would?

ROLE-SWITCHING
(ALL AGES)

Role-switching is thinking from another person's point of view. In role-switching, each person takes a side in a debate. He argues for that side, then switches and argues from the opposite viewpoint. Role-switching can be used as a practice for thinking or used with real-life situations.

How to Use Role-switching

Callie and her dad decided to do a role-switching about which fast-food restaurant had the best food. Dad always wanted to go to Burger King. Callie preferred McDonald's.

When choosing a subject for a role-switching, pick subjects your child is likely to feel strongly about. Which brand of toothpaste is best? Which cartoon character is funniest? Should kids be forced to wear coats in the winter? For adolescents, pick a more complex idea. Should the U.S. trust the USSR? Is it right or wrong for Christians to block the doors at abortion clinics to stop clients from entering the building? Is it wise for Christians to date non-Christians?

Callie and her dad had chosen their sides. Each told three reasons why his or her belief was the best. Callie said McDonalds had better fries, thicker shakes, and neat toys in the kid's meals. Dad said Burger King had better hamburgers, they served onion rings, and they sold Pepsi. After each had stated three points, they switched positions. Callie had to argue for Burger King, and Dad had to argue for McDonald's. That was harder, but both found three good things to say about his or her new side. Dad said many prices were better at McDonald's, the service was fast, and they had good salads. Callie said the playground at Burger King was neat, they let customers pour their own pop, and the hamburgers didn't have onions.

When role-switching, see how completely you and your child understand the position you do not normally support. Talk over how well you defended the other's side. What did you and your child learn? Did she come to a new understanding? Did switching sides force her to deal with information she had been ignoring? Are the arguments on both sides clearer in her mind?

Callie and her dad came to an agreement that both McDonald's and Burger King were good places to eat. They found they enjoyed certain things at each place.

Role-switching will help your child think logically about the entire issue under debate. During a debate, ideas must be expressed in an organized way. Switching to the other side will help her understand the views of another. Taking both positions allows her to gather, sort, and choose using new information. It also requires thinking about thinking. To argue convincingly for another side, your child must be prepared to set aside prejudices. Role-switching is a good test of your child's thinking skills.

Real-life Role-switching

Callie and her father also used role-switching in real-life confrontations. They used it to discuss why Callie should keep her room clean. Switching sides helped Callie to understand a little better why her parents objected to the chaos in her room. Here are some other issues that can be used for discussion: Is it important to raise a low math grade? Is it okay for Christians to date non-Christians? Should teenagers have to obey their parents?

Role-switching can sometimes diffuse tense arguments. It can actually be funny to argue for something you believe in strongly, then arguing against it two minutes later. If the issue is not very important, role-switching can reveal how silly it is to fight. Try it the next time your children have a battle. You can be the referee.

SIMULATION ACTIVITIES
(ALL AGES)

Have you ever seen a flight simulator? Flight simulators are airplane cockpits on the ground. They have real controls which move them up and down and from side to side. The pilot's window is a television screen which shows what would happen in a real flight. Pilots and pilots-in-training use them to learn how to fly airplanes better. In a simulator, pilots can crash hundreds of times and still walk away without a scratch. They are as close to real life as possible. Yet they save men and women every day from disaster.

Simulation activities give your child a chance to pilot his way through a real-life decision without real-life consequences. He will go through all the steps of making real choices, but his choices only affect the simulation, not his life.

How to Use Simulation

Simulation activities center around real choices. Theo wanted to buy a car. His mom decided to help him by simulating that choice. She went with him to look at a car he wanted to buy, and they found out how much it would cost. Then she helped Theo shop around for a loan. Theo's next step was to call agents about insurance rates.

Using play money, Mom paid Theo his monthly salary. He had to give her back the money for his car payment and insurance. After they estimated the average cost of maintenance and gas, he had to give her that money too. Then he calculated the cost of his other expenses. After Theo counted what was left, he had to ask himself if he could afford to buy the car he wanted and maintain it. He decided he needed a cheaper car or a better job.

Mom went through the same steps with her younger child, Summer. Summer wanted to buy a toy car for her Barbie. She and her mom priced the item. Mom counted out Summer's allowance in play money, then they estimated how many weeks Summer needed to save to afford the toy car she wanted.

Simulation can be applied to other situations. It can be helpful in choosing a college or a career. Simulation can be used to act out emergencies in your home, such as fires or injuries. Simulation is most effective if you make the pretend experience real enough to require Wisdom Thinking.

Think It Over

Simulation allows your child to test his thinking. How well would he do in real life? Talk about his performance. What did he learn? What adjustments will he have to make next time to do well in real life?

THINKING GAMES
(ALL AGES)

Most kids enjoy playing board and card games. And many commercially produced games, new and old, can be used to teach thinking skills. This makes them a good investment. And games are something the whole family can do together.

The list of games below are arranged by the type of skill they teach. They are not grouped by age or ability level. So check the games carefully for suggested age levels of players before you buy.

Counting, following directions: *Chutes & Ladders*; *Candyland*

Memory development: *Memory* (*Animal Families, Locomotion; Advanced versions* also available)

Using "inside" information: *Pictionary* (*Junior* version available); *Win, Lose, or Draw* (*Junior* version available)

Sorting letters to make words: *Scrabble* (*Junior* version available); *Word Yahtzee*; *Boggle* (*Junior* version available); *Perquacky*

Sorting and choosing: *Guess Who*; *Clue* (*Master Detective* and *video versions* also available)

Strategy games: *Connect Four*; *Checkers*; *Risk*; *Battleship*; *Sorry*

Money management choices: *Monopoly*; *Payday*

Matching and sorting: *Dominoes*; *Uno*; *Bingo*; *Solitaire* (card game)

Real-life choices: *Life*; *Payday*

Using Games with Your Child

Some of these games are quite structured (*Candyland, Chutes & Ladders, Bingo*). The outcome of the game does not depend much on the skill of the players. Others are games of skill and strategy. If you play with your child, you can teach her some of the more difficult thinking that will help her master the skill involved. You can use word games such as *Boggle* and *Perquacky* to teach letter groupings which can be transferred from one word to make other new words (basic spelling). Games such as *Guess Who* and *Clue* teach the process of elimination, but many kids need help getting started with that concept.

If you have a computer in your home, find out what games are available on compatible software. Some games allow kids to choose their own outcomes to adventure stories. They are similar to the "choose your own adventure" books. Others teach matching and sorting skills. Informational games help to increase "outside" knowledge. Computer skills are also good preparation for school today and work in the future.

So play with your child. Teach her skills through games. Make thinking fun. Plan some playful thinking times at your house.

YOU TRY IT!

Playacting

Help your child to think and to observe thinking while acting out a part in a short play. Choose a problem to solve or an idea to investigate. Try to have a wise character and a foolish character. Then choose a cast, props, and a theater. Plan for playacting by filling out the form below. Let the show begin!

What's the Problem? or What is the Idea?

_____

_____

_____

Who are the characters?

_____

_____

_____

What are the props?

_____

_____

_____

Where will the play take place?

_____

_____

_____

What is the Script?

Write out a script for each character. Or better yet, just a few ideas you want each character to follow. Who will act wise? Who will act foolish? How does the play start? How does it end? What happens in the middle?

Beginning

_____

_____

_____

_____

Middle

_____

_____

_____

_____

End

_____

_____

_____

_____

Describe what character one is like, how character one usually acts.

_____

_____

Describe what character two is like, how character two usually acts.

_____

_____

Describe what character three is like, how character three usually acts.

_____

_____

When the Curtain falls. You all are the play-acting critics. Ask yourselves these five questions:

1. How did you like the play?

2. Who was a Wisdom Thinker? How could you tell? What was the result of the character's wise thinking?

3. Who was foolish? How could you tell he or she was foolish? What was the result of the character's foolish thinking?

4. What changes could the foolish character make in his or her thinking?

5. Who is most like you?

Role-Playing

Have your older child take on the role of an expert thinker. To do this, he will need to create his own script after researching his character.

Who is the expert thinker?

_____

What did the expert thinker do?

_____

_____

_____

_____

_____

_____

_____

_____

_____

_____

What other characters were part of the expert thinkers life?

_____

_____

_____

What is the Script?

Your older child should be the one who writes script for each character. Once again, he or she can write out just a few ideas you want each character to follow. Who will act wise? Who will act foolish? How does the play start? How does it end? What happens in the middle?

Beginning

_____

_____

_____

_____

_____

Middle

_____

_____

_____

_____

_____

End

_____

_____

_____

_____

_____

Individual scripts. Write out individual scripts on separate sheets of paper for each of the characters.

What are the props?

1. _____

2. _____

3. _____

4. _____

Where will the play take place?

1. _____

2. _____

3. _____

When the Curtain falls. Your older child is the critic. Have him or her ask these five questions.

1. How did you like the play?

2. What were the best aspects of the expert thinker's character?

3. What were the weaknesses of the expert thinker?

4. What changes could the expert thinker make in his or her thinking?

5. How are you like the expert thinker? How are you different?

Role-Switching

Have your child of any age choose one side of an issue. They can start out being for it or against it—let them choose. Have another child or yourself take the other side. After both sides have told their ideas, change sides.

The Issue

_____

_____

_____

Who is for the issue?

_____

Who is against it?

_____

Five reasons why you are for the issue.

1. _____
2. _____
3. _____
4. _____
5. _____

Five reasons why you are against the issue.

1. _____
2. _____

3. _____

4. _____

5. _____

The Plan for the Discussion

Round One

Person One: Five reasons for the issue

Person Two: Disagreements to one or more of the five reasons

Break—five-minute break to plan for round two

Round Two

Person Two: Five reasons against the issue

Person One: Disagreements to one or more of the five reasons

Switch sides.

Now repeat round one and round two from the other side.

Together decide which ideas are best and which are worst. Does the other side have some good points? What have you learned about your thinking? What have you learned about their thinking?

Simulation Activities

Simulation activities are about choices. They are making choices just like in real life, but without the real-life consequences. Have your child decide on something they want to do, to be, or to buy. Now go through the following steps of a simulation and make a choice.

What will you do, be, or buy?

_____

Where will you get information for your choice? (You may want to read the Method on Bible Search and Research first for some ideas). You should list experts and printed materials.

1. _____
2. _____
3. _____
4. _____

List the pros and cons of the information you gathered for your choice.

Pros

1. _____
2. _____
3. _____
4. _____
5. _____

Cons

1. _____
2. _____
3. _____
4. _____
5. _____

What did you choose?

1. _____

Are you happy with your choice? Was your gathering of information complete? What could you have done differently? Did you gather, sort, and choose, all the time thinking about your thinking and thinking about God? Would you recommend your choice to someone else?

Thinking Games

Select a game from those listed above. Why not include the whole family. Make some popcorn. Have some fun!

What game do you plan to play?

_____

When are you going to play it?

_____

Have each player tell one thing they noticed about their own thinking and one thing they noticed about another player's thinking. Be positive. Reward good thinking.

Player One about himself

_____

Player One about another

_____

Player Two about himself

_____

Player Two about another

_____

Player Three about himself

_____

Player Three about another

_____

Player Four about himself

_____

Player Four about another

_____

CHAPTER NINE

Storytelling

Nothing captures the mind of a child more than a good story. Whether fiction or truth, stories have the power to touch the deepest emotions. They can engage the imagination as they communicate facts and ideas, and they make the hearer think about concepts he might never have thought of before.

We're all familiar with folk and fairy tales passed down from one generation to another. But two other kinds of storytelling are common as well: oral history and storybooks. All three types of stories can be used to teach thinking.

ORAL HISTORY

Sarah and Josh love to visit my mother-in-law, Doris. In fact they are usually reluctant to come home because she really throws herself into being a grandma. All three of them try to squeeze as much as they can out of every second they're together.

One of the best things about Grandma Doris is that she tells lots of stories about her family. My kids never knew her father, Clarence, but he comes alive in mischievous splendor as they giggle over stories about him and his wife Signe.

Clarence loved to eat anything and everything. But Signe was into health foods in a big way, and she did a lot of policing of Clarence's diet. Whenever they came to visit at Doris's house, Clarence would wait until the two women were settled into a long discussion. Then he would nonchalantly inch toward the kitchen where he raided the forbidden cookie jar filled with Oreos. When his mouth was stuffed full, Signe would catch him. Foiled again!

My kids feel as if they were there as Grandma recalls toiling through nurse's training. And as she paints verbal pictures of a small two-room apartment in Chicago, they see a little bit of what their daddy's early years were like. Through her oral history, Sarah and Josh have a firm link to the past. And they are gathering information for thinking and choice making they'll probably never forget.

Oral history is the oldest form of storytelling. These accounts of past events are rarely written down. Most exist only in human memories—of the person who lived them or of a person to whom the story was told. Family history is a great way to teach choosing. Most kids enjoy it because it is special "inside" knowledge. Because it really happened, personal history often has a greater impact than warnings or made-up tales.

How to Use Oral History to Teach Thinking

The beauty of oral history is that we all have some stories of the past to tell. You have a history to share with your child, and your past is most likely full of stories about choices, both wise and foolish. You can use this powerful tool by following these six suggestions.

Relate the past to the present. Children are occupied with the present. They think about what's happening to them right now. The past may be interesting to them, but usually only when it relates to their own experience. If your son is just starting first grade, talk about your own fears about school: new teachers, mean kids, or wearing the wrong clothes. Tell him how it worked out and how you solved your problems. If your daughter is a teen, tell her about your feelings, crushes, and complexion problems.

Choose your stories carefully. Make sure the story fits the situation and is right for your child's age. If you want to talk about getting along, don't tell about the time you solved a dispute with your brother by bashing him over the head with a baseball bat.

Sometimes it is tempting to try to teach a principle in abstract terms. "God will take care of you" can be conveyed in several ways. You could sing the song "His Eye Is on the Sparrow," or you could talk about the lilies of the field and how they neither toil nor spin. But a younger child might benefit more from hearing how God supplied your needs even when your dad was out of work and your family had no money for food. It would mean even more if he could understand that you didn't get an allowance for six months. Unless you are sure your child can generalize and transfer ideas like an adult, stick to simple messages.

Tell about your failures and what you learned. It's important to be honest with children. None of us are super-heroes. Successes are easy to talk about, but when we admit failures, we show our children we are learners too. And children can relate to us more easily when we show our weaknesses. Sarah and I have had many talks about the perils of "getting back" at others who have hurt us. I've told her about my anger at some of my friends and some of the cruel things I did to hurt them. We've talked about the pain my actions caused, not only to those I meant to hurt, but also to myself.

Admitting a boo-boo shows that if you survived, your child will survive too. But don't stop with admitting failure. Tell what happened after your thinking mistake. If you shoplifted as a youth, tell what happened. Did you get caught? If not, how did you live with the guilt? Follow the story through to the end to help your child learn from the consequences of your actions.

Try not to moralize. Let the story tell the story. Storytellers who go into a three-point final argument lose their listeners. I've often seen my kids and my students at school drift off when the "action" part of the story was over. Kids respond best to brief endings. If they want more explanation, they'll usually ask. And if less is said, they often want more.

Keep it real. Children can usually guess when the truth is being padded. We need to resist the temptation to make up juicy details. Your life may seem boring to you, but remember, your child didn't live it. Most children just love to hear about their parents when they were young.

Use oral history to solve and prevent problems. It's amazing how similar our child's present experiences can be to our past ones. But often kids do not ask for advice because they believe their parents couldn't possibly understand. "You never liked a boy who didn't like you," daughters often wail to their mothers. Personal stories bridge the gap between generations. The look of wonder on my daughter's face when I tell her, "That happened to me, too" is the evidence of my need to share.

Oral history can also be used to warn children of the results of poor choices. But beware of romanticizing "sowing wild oats" stories. That can backfire. Soft-pedaling sin benefits no one. Told seriously, however, your warnings can have great impact. Even if they do not totally deter your child from wrong choices, remembering your story may be enough to lead her back before greater damage is done.

CLASSIC STORYTELLING

At our house my husband is the creative storyteller. John has a fertile and silly imagination which works to his advantage. He enjoys weaving tales for our children, the more outrageous, the better.

We recently went to a river and watched the fishermen, and our children were amazed by the piles of tangled fishing line on the shore. John made up a story to explain this:

> Billy the Worm was dug out of the ground by a mean little boy. Billy thought all was lost when he was stuck on a hook and thrown into the river. Along came Sammy the Fish. He was just about to bite into Billy, but Billy, being a smart little worm, warned Sammy that there was a mean little boy at the end of the line who wanted Sammy for dinner. So Sammy gently released Billy from the hook with his nimble fish lips, and the two of them joined together to tangle the mean little boy's fishing line on a nearby log. Sammy gave Billy a ride to the shore, and both got away from their awful fate.

The advantage of classic storytelling is that it can be made to fit your child's needs and circumstances. When your child has a problem, you can make up an imaginary character (much like your child) who will face a similar dilemma in your story. Or you can pick a well-known, age-old tale to tell and modify it for the occasion. John used an Aesop's storytelling style in the Billy and Sammy story.

Stories don't have to be polished, professional entertainment. I'm not nearly as good at making up stories on-the-spot as my husband is. But I've found that my kids are more than willing to listen to my feeble attempts. They appreciate my stories even with their little pauses while I figure out what to say next. I think kids just like to hear from their parents through stories. And they often aren't as critical of us as we are of ourselves.

How to Use Storytelling to Teach Thinking

Make up stories that fit your child. Trudy likes to tell stories to her daughter, Chloe. She starts by focusing on Chloe's major concerns. One day it might be friendships, another day it's peer pressure or acceptance. Trudy also thinks about her daughter's primary interests. Chloe likes music, sports, and school work. When Trudy devises a story, she makes it similar to Chloe's concerns and interests so she can relate closely to the characters. Chloe often likes to be the star of the story. Your child might like that too.

You can also choose subjects that are unlike your child's situation, but be sure it fits her interest and maturity level. Stories can widen horizons. Use them to acquaint her with new ideas.

Figure out a beginning, middle, and ending. The best storytellers have a plan. Garrison Keillor, whose outstanding tale-spinning talents were showcased on "A Prairie Home Companion," works out a basic framework for all his stories. Though he may seem to ramble in the middle, he always ties it up neatly at the end. A framework allows for creativity, yet keeps the story moving in the right direction.

Trudy finds that it's easiest to plan ahead. She starts with a problem to solve or an idea to investigate.

One day she thought up the story of Andrea, who told her friends she went to Europe for her summer vacation. Andrea chose to tell her fib to impress her friends. But since she hadn't really been to Europe, she was sure to be caught sooner or later. Andrea would then experience the consequences. Sound familiar? It's Wisdom Thinking Walt Disney-style.

Trudy knows where she's going with her story, she embellishes it and makes it fun. She does this by making some of the choices obviously wrong. She also makes some choices silly. In her vacation story, Andrea tells all her friends about Europe, but one friend does not believe her. She has a chance to tell the truth, but she doesn't. Finally one of the friends blurts out in social studies class that Andrea knows all about France because she was there last summer. But—surprise—Andrea doesn't know any more than the rest of the class. The truth comes out in front of thirty witnesses, totally embarrassing Andrea.

When Trudy first told stories to Chloe, she was sure to make one choice obviously good. As Trudy became a better storyteller, and Chloe became a better listener, Trudy made some of the choices vague. This has helped Chloe to do some careful thinking.

Length is important. Remember, some children can listen to stories for long periods while others need stories no longer than TV commercials. When a story involves your child, he may sit still for longer than usual. But before fatigue shows, end the story. It's better to drop the curtain early than to bore the audience.

Try storytelling variations. Kids love to add their own two cents to stories. You can let your child help out with good results. Try starting a story with one or two lines, then let your child tell the next part. Make it simple like: "A man went out to the store to buy some M & M's. On the way he saw a cat stuck up in a tree." Then let your child take up the story. Go back and forth between the two of you and see how the cat gets rescued. You can learn a lot about how your child thinks by working on stories together like this. Of course, other family members can also participate. It helps if your kids are used to hearing stories before you try this. Then they will have some idea of the beginning, middle, and end.

You can also tell a story up to a certain point—perhaps when the character must make a decision—then stop. Tell about the man climbing the tree, getting stuck himself with no one to help. Then have your child pick up the tale. Let her finish it with the choice made and the consequences.

A third variation is a "choose your own adventure" format. You start the story, but at every place where a choice must be made, your child makes the decision. The man goes out for M & M's. He sees the cat. What does he do? Your child can choose if he helps the cat or goes on to the store. You then tell what happens next based on her choice, and then go on to the next dilemma. She chooses again and again. This type of story can be very realistic. She makes the choices, you control the consequences.

Balance the fun and the teaching. Stories aren't fun if they're too message-laden. Story time should be relaxing and intimate. Children who sense that the storyteller has a "hidden agenda" don't like it much. It's a good idea to limit the number of thinking principles to one or two per story to prevent overkill. Fewer principles will also help her remember what she learned.

READING STORYBOOKS

As a grade school librarian, I have many opportunities to promote reading with children and parents. I try to do so every chance I get because I believe in the power of books to change lives. I'm thrilled to see mothers with young children checking out books to read at home, not only because they're encouraging reading, but because they are also teaching their children to think.

How to Use Books to Teach Thinking

Most stories for kids are filled with characters making choices. (What will Tim do next? Will Tanya take her good friend's advice?) Much of the fun in "fun books" centers around thinking mistakes. We laugh at the trouble caused by a poor choice or mix-up. Learning to understand these thinking mistakes is a way of learning to think.

When I read to my children, we often talk about the choices made in the story. If a character steals to get something they want, I ask my kids to think about what other choices the character had. We enjoy trying to predict what will happen next because of the decision made. Sarah likes to put herself in the same situation. What would she do?

We also think about thinking while we're reading. It's not hard to spot thinking errors made by the characters. Sometimes we see they didn't look at all their choices before they made a snap decision.

Even young kids can recognize when characters didn't listen to wise advice.

There are so many things to talk about when we read together! But I've found that asking too many questions can be distracting. When I ask too many questions my kids say, "Oh, Mom, can't we just read the story?" But if your child is willing, ask at least one or two thinking questions during every story you read.

After years of asking thinking questions, I've found that my children like to ask questions too. When they do, I have them try to answer their own question first. Many times they are on the right track and I can take the opportunity to say, "Good thinking." Sometimes they can see part of the picture, and together we make it whole.

Choose stories carefully. When I look for books at the public library for Sarah and Josh, I'm picky. I want stories that are right for their reading level and interests. I don't want books that are too young, or my kids lose interest. On the other hand, I am cautious of stories that are too advanced for my kids. Otherwise we might find ourselves caught smack dab in the middle of a teen romance before we know what hit us. I've found that most children like books about kids who are their age or just a little older. Carefully previewed, books about older kids can be a good step forward for both the reader and the hearer.

Length is also important in choosing stories. Up through second grade, children like little stories with lots of pictures. But some can handle longer story times than others. My two kids were totally different in the amount of time they would allow me to read to them. Sarah would sit down and listen whenever I had the time. Josh was interested, but if the story didn't move quickly, he'd simply take off. Both love stories, but on their own terms.

Stories can be done in installments. Kids can learn to exercise their memories by trying to remember details from day to day. With the fifth through eighth graders in library class, we often read books over four or five class periods. We reviewed at the start of each class and covered only a couple of chapters a session. The students then wrote a short paper at the end of each class about what they heard. Both of these exercises helped students remember the details of the story.

Choose a variety of stories. Thinking can be taught through all kinds of literature. Heavy, message-laden dramatic fiction is not the only kind of story that teaches thinking. Choice making can also be taught through silly stories and make-believe. Biographies, nature tales, fantasy, and poetry are all great for teaching thinking and choosing. Storytelling that is too intense ceases to be enjoyable. One year I read three books, one after the other, to the sixth grade class. All were realistic stories about children growing up under less-than-ideal conditions. Though the kids were interested in all three books, we all agreed by the end of the last book that we were ready for something lighter. Have fun.

Preview the books available. Hundreds of children's books are published each year. The variety of subjects they cover is astounding. If you are near a public library, you should never lack for books you can use to teach your child about making choices.

Many libraries give out recommended reading lists for children. In addition, Jim Trelease's *Read-Aloud Handbook* is an excellent guide for finding good books for children of all ages. *Honey for a Child's Heart* by Gladys Hunt and *How to Grow a Young Reader* by John and Kathryn Lindskoog are also helpful for choosing high-quality literature. Ask friends, teachers, and librarians for assistance in finding the kinds of books you want. Book reviews are also helpful. But as with any recommendation, preview the book first before using it with your child.

When your child reads on her own. At some point, your child will read mostly on her own. Sarah and Josh have been at that stage for quite a while. But I think you can still teach thinking through books. I often ask my kids about what they're reading. Since we talked over books from the time they were small, they still analyze them alone the way we did together.

I know many children do not want to talk about what they read. Some just don't prefer this kind of conversation. But I encourage you to try to talk with your child about the content of the books he reads. Maybe having a family book-sharing time would help. Each family member could talk about a book they have read and would like to recommend to the rest of the family. The effort to talk about content is important. It's too easy to absorb ideas and find behaviors acceptable when reading without discernment.

Of course, we cannot know for sure what is going on in a book unless we take the time to read it ourselves. At least we should be familiar with the track record of the author. By all means, if we've heard other parents make disparaging remarks about certain books, we should find out why. We need to be aware of what our children check out from the library, buy for themselves, and borrow from friends.

All kinds of stories can be powerful tools to teach thinking. With a little planning, we can make books a gateway to good thinking. If we use them wisely, we will be greatly rewarded.

YOU TRY IT!

Oral History

Oral history is special "inside" knowledge. It tells what really happened to someone we know or knew. It's personal history and often has a greater impact on what we decide to believe or do than warnings or made-up tales.

About whom or what are you going to tell a story?

_____

How does the story relate to the present? What current problems will it solve or prevent?

_____

What are the successful thinking episodes in the story?

_____

_____

_____

_____

What are the thinking failures in the story?

_____

_____

_____

_____

How will the story begin?

_____

_____

_____

_____

_____

_____

_____

What happens in the middle of the story?

_____

_____

_____

_____

_____

_____

_____

How does the story end?

_____

_____

_____

_____

_____

_____

_____

How did the hearer like the story? What did you like about your storytelling? What do you want to change next time?

Classic Storytelling

Classic storytelling can be made to fit your child's needs. When your child has a problem, you can make up an imaginary character (much like your child) who will face a similar dilemma in your story.

What problem or dilemma is your child facing?

_____

_____

_____

Is there a traditional story or tale you can adapt for this situation?

yes_____ no_____

If there is a traditional story or tale you can adapt, what is the title of the story? Or what is the title of your new, imaginary story?

_____

194

Who are the main characters? And what are they like?

Character One

_____

_____

Character Two

_____

_____

Character Three

_____

_____

Where does the story take place?

_____

How will the story begin?

_____

_____

_____

_____

_____

_____

_____

What happens in the middle of the story?

_____

_____

_____

_____

_____

_____

_____

How does the story end?

_____

_____

_____

_____

_____

_____

Where in the story can your child contribute?
What can he or she contribute?

_____

_____

_____

_____

What's the moral of the story?

_____

_____

_____

_____

How did it go? Was the story fun and helpful? What would you do differently next time?

_____

_____

_____

_____

_____

_____

_____

Story Books

Most stories for kids are filled with characters making choices. Learning to understand the choices and mistakes of characters in a story is a fun way of learning to think.

What is the title of the book?

_____

Are you going to do all of the reading or are you going to share the reading with other family members?

_____

When you sense that an episode in the story is over, stop and fill in the blanks below:

Who is the main character you want to observe?

_____

What did this character do? Encourage a brief summary and not the retelling of the entire story.

_____

_____

_____

_____

_____

What thinking and choices caused the character to do the things you just listed in the question above?

_____

_____

_____

_____

_____

Do you think the character acted wisely?

yes_____ no_____

Could wisdom thinking have changed the character's actions? How could it have changed the character's actions?

_____

_____

_____

_____

_____

CHAPTER TEN

Controlled Experience

In the early evening, Sarah, Josh, and I like to ride our bikes. Our two-mile ride is fun. It's also good exercise. But in addition to these more obvious benefits, Sarah and Josh learn to think as we pedal around.

Our neighborhood bustles with people and everything that goes with them: pets, bikes, skateboards, motorcycles, and especially cars. So as we ride, my kids must think carefully in order to safely negotiate the maze of obstacles. It isn't an easy task. Around every corner lurks a new hazard. The thinking that is required tests my children's Wisdom Thinking skills. And because I am with them watching over their thinking, our family bike rides are *controlled experiences*.

WHAT IS A CONTROLLED EXPERIENCE?

A controlled experience is any situation where your child can practice Wisdom Thinking *with your supervision.* Your child is allowed to test his thinking skill. He makes choices, but you watch the whole process. If he needs your help, you are there to give it.

A controlled experience can be as simple as our family bike ride, or it can be as complex as investigating a moral issue. When you sit beside your teenager in the car as he learns to drive, that is a controlled experience. So is observing your children as they work together to solve a disagreement. All of these experiences share in common the exercise of Wisdom Thinking skills coupled with the overseeing, helpful presence of an older, wiser thinker.

The Advantages of a Controlled Experience

Controlled experiences are the best opportunities for children to practice the three skills of Wisdom Thinking. Denise went hiking with her parents. Dad had prepared Denise by reading maps with her and talking about signs on the trail. They planned a hike together to test her skills in a controlled experience. Dad watched as Denise made choices at each fork in the trail and he jogged her memory if she forgot to check the map before making decisions. Mom encouraged Denise by remarking how well she was choosing for all of them. Dad anticipated difficulties. Knowing what lay ahead, he allowed Denise to make a few mistakes he knew would not endanger them. Since Denise discovered her mistakes, he didn't have to step in and correct her. But, if necessary, Dad and Mom could have saved Denise from the results of any poor choices.

The Safety Benefit

Safety is a great benefit of controlled experience. Denise could have taken a wrong turn and gotten lost, or even worse, fallen off a cliff. But with her dad and mom along, she was safe making the choices. When my children go riding with me, I watch them constantly. I can tell by their actions if they are gathering, sorting, and choosing wisely. At times, one of my kids will completely abandon awareness of oncoming cars. The other may drift into the middle of the street. Since I am there, I can remind them to think ahead and get near the curb, out of the way of danger. My warning helps my children get their thoughts back on track. And it saves them from accidents.

Controlled experiences can also save your child from emotional or spiritual accidents. As your child works through a problem, you can guide her thinking to wiser choices. Amanda and Kara, next-door neighbors, had been good friends, but now they weren't getting along. Their moms didn't intervene much at first. They hoped the girls would work out their problems on their own. But days went by and little progress was made toward renewed friendship. Then the girls started to devise plans to "get back" at each other. At that point, Amanda's mom and Kara's mom put their heads together. They agreed it was time to step in and help the girls solve their problems.

The girls were brought together, and their moms encouraged them to pray. Then Amanda and Kara gathered information from each other.

Amanda broke the ice by saying, "I heard from Rachel that you don't like me anymore."

"I never said that," Kara quickly replied. "Rachel told me you didn't like being with me!"

Amanda thought for a minute. "Maybe I did tell Rachel I was mad at you. But it was because you made a big deal about your new stereo. I was jealous."

"I never made a big deal about it," said Kara.

Kara's mom interjected, "Kara, it was all you talked about for days after you got it. Maybe you weren't thinking about how Amanda was feeling."

"Well, maybe I did say too much. I didn't mean to make you jealous. I was just excited," said Kara.

Amanda's mom said, "I think we can all understand that. It is exciting to get something that special."

Kara and Amanda continued to sort through their feelings.

Their mothers helped them see that their emotions had distorted their thinking. Then the girls thought about how to obey God in this relationship. Finally, with a little motherly assistance, they chose to be friends again. In a controlled experience, we can help our children avoid the harm caused by unwise choices.

The Practice Benefit

Controlled experiences provide opportunities to practice Wisdom Thinking skills over and over again. You learned in chapter 7 that practice is necessary to use the skills well. And controlled experiences are the best way to give your child quality practice time.

The value of practice is maximized during controlled experience because we are there to spot errors and correct them as they occur. If our child makes a poor decision, she may not be able to figure out what caused her bad choice without some help from us. Left to think on her own, she may make that same thinking mistake over and over again. But if we spend some time with her in a controlled experience, we may easily see her error. Then we can help her to correct it.

Remember the master craftsmen with the "wise" hands I told you about earlier? They were shadowed day and night by apprentices eager to learn their craft. The masters didn't give them a lecture or two and then let them loose in a room full of gold and olive wood. They spent years working side by side until the apprentices proved their skill.

You are your child's master thinker. Your child is your thinking apprentice. Controlled experiences will give your child the one-to-one training she needs to develop and refine her Wisdom Thinking skills.

HOW A CONTROLLED EXPERIENCE WORKS

You and your child both have important roles in a controlled experience. The parent is both a coach and a lifeguard. The child is the athlete-thinker.

Your Role as Coach

If you've ever watched sports on television you've seen coaches in action. They pace the sidelines at the edge of the action. Sometimes they yell encouragement. They often talk to their team between plays. Other times they just watch. To the casual observer, they seem to play a minor role in the team's win or loss. But game time is just a small part of a coach's job. What the coach does every day in practice makes the difference between winning and losing on game night.

During the week the coach teaches his team to play the game skillfully. Part of his teaching is going over the rules, but mostly he helps his players develop the skills necessary to play the game well. He does this by going through a teaching routine. First, the coach shows his player the skill he wants the player to learn. Second, the coach watches as the player tries to imitate the actions. Third, the coach corrects any mistakes the player makes. This cycle of show-watch-correct, show-watch-correct, is repeated over and over again. As weeks go by, the player gets better and better at his new skill.

As thinking coaches, we also teach our child the rules of Wisdom Thinking. We explain how to be a skillful gatherer, sorter, and chooser. We tell him how to think about thinking. We make sure he knows how to think about God. But for our child to develop those skills, we need to go through the same teaching routine the sports coach uses. We begin by showing him how to use a thinking skill. If we're working on gathering, we show him how to gather, then we watch as he tries to imitate us. We see how well he does, and then we correct any gathering mistakes we see. Then we show, watch, and correct again.

During controlled experiences, you'll be right there with your child practicing every day. And those daily practices will pay off. When the day of the big game comes, you'll be able to stand on the sidelines watching your best player show his skillful thinking.

Your Role as Lifeguard

During a controlled experience, we also act as our children's lifeguard. As our kids practice their thinking, we need to keep a watchful eye on them. They may begin to flounder in the sea of facts, ideas, and choices. They may not use every thinking skill correctly. But we need to let our kids have a chance to put their skills to work. Sometimes they may benefit most from hearing our encouraging words. As hard as it is, we shouldn't rush in to save them before they have a chance to try to save themselves.

However, if you see your child gasping for air and ready to go under, be there with a helping hand. If your daughter begins flirting with the guy in school with the worst reputation, step in and help her rethink her choice. If your son wants to drop out of school because it isn't any fun, help him make a better choice. If your child is in danger of making a dangerous choice, don't hesitate to intervene. Dive in when she needs to be rescued!

Your Child as Athlete-Thinker

Your young thinker has an important role in a controlled experience too. That role is to be the mental athlete. He will practice using Wisdom Thinking skills under your watchful eye.

When you're looking for a controlled experience to use with your child, look for practical situations where both of you will be present. Shopping trips, family travels, research for school papers, and reviewing movies are all experiences that can be planned in advance to test thinking skill. Or a controlled experience can be quite spontaneous. When your child comes to you with a problem or you're in the middle of an amusement park, let her do the thinking while you coach.

April had too many toys. In fact, it was hard to find a path to her bed at night. So April's parents decided it was time to weed out the overflowing collection and give some of it away. They used this situation as a controlled experience.

They suggested their idea to April. At first she wasn't wild about giving her toys away, but after talking with her parents, she decided it would be nice to let other kids enjoy some of the toys she had owned for a long time.

April began gathering her toys and sorting them into two piles. On one pile she stacked the toys she would consider giving away; the other pile had toys she wanted to keep. She would put them away when the give-away toys were gone. This was her own idea, and her parents felt it was wise.

After the toys were separated, April asked what she should do next. She wasn't sure she wanted to give away all the older toys—she would never see them again! Dad suggested she sort through them and decide if she wanted to give some to friends or younger children she knew. April liked that idea.

As she sorted, she thought about kids who didn't have any toys at all. She wondered if she was being selfish. God would be happy if she gave some of her nicer things away too, she thought. April talked to Mom about her idea and they prayed together. They also looked up some verses about giving and loving one another. April decided to go back and check her "save" pile. She transferred a few newer toys to the "give away" group.

Finally, her sorting was done. Mom and Dad came in to check her choices. They talked about some of the toys she had chosen to give away. April realized she had made a choosing error by planning to give away her oldest stuffed bunny that Grandma had made for her. She put it in her "save" pile. Her parents questioned her about other toys, but she had good reasons for discarding them. Her parents agreed with her reasons. Together the family dropped off the toys April had chosen to donate to friends and charity. She was happy with her choice when she saw the smiles on the faces of those who received her toys.

How Your Child Benefits

Skills learned through controlled experiences can help your child in two ways. First, it will help when she needs to make the same decisions without your help. April will probably run her own home some day, and she'll need to clean it out now and then and give away unusable items. She was allowed to do most of the gathering, sorting, and choosing with her toys as a child. As an adult, she'll be better prepared to sort through old clothes, toasters, and golf clubs in the future.

Second, April can transfer the skills she learned to other situations. Gathering and sorting usable and unusable toys is a lot like gathering and sorting usable and unusable facts. The skill is the same, it is simply applied to another situation. As your child matures, she will be able to transfer skills more easily.

REVIEW YOUR CONTROLLED EXPERIENCE

With a controlled experience, it is wise to go back and think over what has happened. Both you and your child should ask yourselves a few questions.

Parent Review

Think about your role as a coach. Did I show, watch, and correct? Was I patient, allowing my child time to master her skill? Did I lecture instead of coach?

Think about your role as a lifeguard. Did I allow my child to try out her skills? Or was I more of a life jacket than a lifeguard?

Child Review

Ask your child if she was a Wisdom Thinker. Did she follow through with her choice? Was it a good choice? Did others agree that the choice was wise?

YOU TRY IT!

A controlled experience is any situation where your child can practice Wisdom Thinking *under supervision.* Your child is allowed to test her thinking skill. She makes choices, but you watch the whole process. If she needs your help, you are there to give it.

The Experience

What problem is your child going to solve, or what idea is he or she going to investigate?

_____

_____

_____

What areas do you think you might jump in and help too quickly? Write them down here and remind yourself to be a lifeguard and not a life jacket.

_____

_____

_____

_____

How are you going to coach your child through the experience?

_____

_____

_____

_____

How did your young Wisdom Thinker do?

_____

_____

_____

_____

How did you do as coach? Did you show the skill and then have your child practice? Or did you find yourself mostly telling?

_____

_____

_____

_____

How did you do as a lifeguard? Were you alert to help without helping when you weren't needed?

_____

_____

_____

_____

CHAPTER ELEVEN

Rethinking

It was after 11:30 p.m. Annie, who had gone to a movie with some girlfriends, had agreed to come home no later than 10:00. But she had not called and her father, Ed, had no idea where she could be. He tried to relax and not think horrible thoughts. Reading a magazine was a hopeless effort. His eyes followed the words, but his brain didn't register their meaning. Every few minutes, Ed rose from his chair and peered out into the night.

A few times he heard cars turn the corner and come down the street. Each time he thought it was Annie, but the cars drove past the house without slowing. Ed looked at his watch and checked it against the clock on the wall. No mistaking, it was late.

Finally, near midnight, he heard another car. Unlike the others, this one stopped in front of the house. A car door opened, and gales of laughter filled the night as Annie said goodbye to her friends.

Ed knew he and Annie needed to talk. They needed to *rethink* some of the choices Annie had made that evening. As her footsteps clicked on the walk, up the steps, and across the porch, Ed prepared to spend some time rethinking Annie's evening with her. The doorknob turned. His daughter was home.

WHAT IS RETHINKING?

Rethinking is talking over thinking and choices after a young thinker has tested her skills. It can follow a good experience where a child made wise choices. Or it can follow a bad experience like Annie's. When we rethink with our child, we can evaluate how well or poorly she formed opinions or made decisions. We can use this review to decide if she should be rewarded for good thinking or corrected for poor thinking.

Rethinking is helpful following a controlled experience. If you do a controlled experience with your child, you'll already know how he thought and made choices. Rethinking will be an important review of what happened. You can use it to correct and to reward.

Other times, as in the case of Annie's dad, you may want to rethink after uncontrolled events. In these situations, parents have no idea how their child did her thinking. We only hear about it after the fact. In uncontrolled experiences rethinking is essential. It may be our only chance to teach our child about what to believe or how to act. Also, it gives us an opportunity to repair damage from bad experiences.

Getting Ready to Rethink

Ed prepared himself for rethinking. He reminded himself that rethinking can be done well if a few simple guidelines are followed.

Emphasize the good. Ed had often used rethinking following Annie's unwise choices or behavior problems. But he also used rethinking after positive events as well. In both situations, he tried to find some good thinking to praise. He wasn't in the mood to praise when Annie came home, but he reminded himself to look for something good to say.

Be a calm teacher. Ed knew his attitude during rethinking would set the tone for the entire session. He tried to calm himself because he wanted to be able to think clearly. It is easy to become overly emotional during a session, especially after an unplanned event such as Annie's late arrival home.

Choose the right time. Ed knew that carefully choosing when to do a rethinking was important. It could help avoid problems. When he and Annie were tired they sometimes did not do well in touchy discussions. If their talk became overly emotional he would set aside another time to talk with Annie. They could talk in the morning or after dinner tomorrow when they might be more relaxed. Annie might be less apt to jump to defend her actions if she had more time to think about her thinking. And both of them might be able to listen more carefully.

When Annie was younger, she couldn't put off talking like she could now. Back then, she wasn't able to remember events after too much time had passed. But this evening, even though it was late, Ed wanted to do a little rethinking while events were still fresh in Annie's mind. And he wanted to tell Annie about the fear he felt for her safety.

Avoid damaging language. The hardest thing for Ed was to remember to think before he spoke. He repeated one of his favorite verses in his mind, "A gentle answer turns away wrath, but a harsh word stirs up anger" (Proverbs 15:1). He didn't want to cast Annie in the role of a "bad kid," because she wasn't. She just made some bad choices sometimes. Ed knew if he called her stupid or dumb, she would believe him, and he never wanted his words to be the reason she gave up trying to do well, or acted out the role of a bad kid for the next few months or years.

Follow a rethinking plan. Ed had a rethinking plan he stuck to each time he did some rethinking with Annie. It gave them both a chance to think and to talk. Ed's plan allowed him to guide the session, but Annie did her own thinking. Ed listened carefully so he knew what was on her mind when she made her choices, then the two of them planned together how to make changes.

A STEP-BY-STEP RETHINKING PLAN

Ed's rethinking times with Annie were not all alike. Some were quick and easy, others were long and involved. If you're doing some rethinking with your child, factors like his age and personality, kind of event, and time limitations will help you decide whether you need to delve in deep or spend only one or two minutes going over thinking behavior. Ed's three-step rethinking plan below can be lengthened or shortened to fit your needs.

Step One—Gather the facts

Ed's first step would be to let Annie tell him about her thinking event.

Dad: I've been worried about you.

Annie: I'm sorry, we were having so much fun, I lost track of the time.

Dad: What were you doing?

Annie: Well, Debbie and I went to get some ice cream after the movie, and there were lots of kids there. None of them were going home at 10:00. Debbie didn't want to leave.

(Dad feels this is most, but not all, of the story.)

Dad: You agreed to be home at 10:00; I assume you knew I'd be worried. Why did you choose to stay out late and not call me?

Annie: Like I said, Debbie didn't want to leave.

Ed asked questions but tried not to make other comments. He wanted to hear the full story from Annie. Ed was convinced she told him the truth. But when we're gathering facts after an uncontrolled event, sometimes we hear reports from others. Other times we're unsure about details. Did we get the whole story? Then we should consider asking another person for input. This may be a friend, teacher, neighbor, or other person who was involved. It's important to make sure they witnessed the event, and in most cases it is best to let our child know we are gathering facts from others. When we're satisfied that we have the complete picture, it's on to Step Two.

Step Two—Sort through thinking together

After Ed had the facts, he planned to ask questions which cover the three elements of Wisdom Thinking.

Dad: You said the reason you weren't on time was because Debbie didn't want to leave. Was there a reason why you didn't want to come home?

Annie: Well, I didn't want the other kids to know I had to be home so soon.

Dad: Is that more the reason than Debbie's wanting to be out late?

Annie: Yes.

Dad: Did you say anything to Debbie about leaving?

Annie: Yes, and she laughed at me.

Dad: I'm glad you asked her, at least. I know it's hard when people make fun of you. Was there anyone else who could have given you a ride home?

Annie: I didn't think about that.

"What went well and why? What went poorly and why?" This is what Ed is trying to discover. He is trying to determine Annie's motive for her choices, then they can discuss the results of her actions. He wanted to find out if she thought ahead to the results of her choices. If Annie had said, "I don't know," to his questions, Ed would have stepped in to lead the conversation with possible answers. He knew it was best to avoid phrases like, "You did this" or "You did that." That shifted the burden of thinking to himself. His goal was to let Annie think about her thinking—Ed wanted her to evaluate her own thoughts. She needed to be aware of her choices.

Step Three—Choose future action

Ed's last step was to help Annie choose her future actions. She had some apologizing and changing she needed to do, and Ed wanted to know how she would behave the next time she was confronted by a similar dilemma.

Dad: We agreed to a time for you to come home and you're very late. What should we do about it?

Annie: I guess I should apologize. I'm sorry Dad, I didn't mean to worry you.

Dad: I accept your apology, but I'm concerned about what you'll do next time.

Annie: It's hard for me to stand up to Debbie. I don't want to seem like a little kid.

Dad: Even adults come home at 10:00. Is there someone else you could go with who would be just as much fun, but who wouldn't pressure you?

Annie: I suppose I could go with Melissa. She leaves earlier than the rest of the kids most of the time, and she doesn't seem to mind if they tease her.

Dad: I think that's a good idea. Is there anything else you can think to do?

Annie: I'll think of you worrying at home. And next time I'll remember to give you a call if I'm going to be a little late.

Dad: Thanks. I worry because I love you.

Annie: I know. I love you too. Are you going to ground me?

Dad: Why don't we talk about it in the morning after we've had some sleep?

Annie: Okay. I'm really tired. Good night, Dad.

After rethinking, Annie needed to apologize for her behavior. This includes asking for God's forgiveness. If circumstances had been different, she may have had to repay someone who had been hurt by her actions. If Annie had been the injured party, Ed would have helped her develop a forgiving spirit. They would have then decided together if she should go and try to resolve the conflict with another person.

Ed and Annie went over changes in thinking that needed to be made next time. They tried to state these changes clearly. Ed made a point of not thinking for Annie. Instead he guided thinking, allowing her ample time to formulate answers of her own. At other times, they used a more direct, step by step approach. Annie would say, "I will make this change, and this is why." A few times, Annie wrote these changes down so she would remember them better. When Annie was younger, Ed simply asked her to repeat these resolutions to him a few times in the next several days. It helped her cement them in her mind.

Last, Ed always tried to give a verbal reward for all wise thinking. He wanted to let Annie know when she made mature choices. It made Annie feel good when she knew her dad was proud of her behavior. Tonight wasn't one of those times, but Ed looked for some good thinking to point out. Ed's rule of thumb when rethinking was: "Reward thinking efforts, punish sin."

This time some punishment would be needed too. But Ed and Annie decided to wait until morning before deciding what it would be. Both of them were too tired to think clearly. The next morning, Ed would let Annie help decide her fate. She'd learned to think wisely about fairness and justice when she was allowed to participate in deciding her own punishment. Often she was harder on herself than Ed would have been.

All in all, it was a successful rethinking. They gathered facts, sorted through thinking, and chose future action. But as you may have noticed, some of the steps mixed into other steps. In normal, relaxed conversation, thoughts often come out randomly rather than step-by-step. The point is, Ed and Annie covered all the bases. Their talk was controlled, Annie did most of the thinking, and they came to an agreement about future action which would improve her thinking next time.

RETHINKING WITH YOUNGER CHILDREN

When rethinking with a younger child, the same steps can be followed. Let's see what happens when Annie's younger brother, Steven, gets in a little trouble of his own the next day.

Mom hears a crash in the family room. She runs in to see her six-year-old, Steven, surrounded by broken glass, looking guilty. He is holding a toy she had taken away from him earlier in the day. She had put it up on a shelf near a vase. After checking to see if he is cut, which he isn't, she begins rethinking:

Gathering the Facts

Mom: What happened?

Steven: The vase fell down.

Mom: I see that. How did it happen?

Steven: I don't know—I guess I knocked it over. I wanted my toy back. I didn't think you'd give it to me, so I got it myself. When I climbed up, the vase fell down and broke.

(Mom recognizes the truth has been told.)

Sorting through Thinking

Mom: Did you think about what might happen before you went to get the toy?

Steven: No.

Mom: Did you do the right thing?

Steven: No. I shouldn't have climbed up on the furniture.

Mom: What else should you have thought of?

Steven: I should have asked you for my toy.

Mom: Right. I took that toy away from you this morning because you were hurting Tim with it. You knew you had to ask me to get it back. Did you want to get it back without me knowing?

Choosing Future Actions

Steven: Yes—I'm sorry.

Mom: Steven, what you did was really dangerous. What could have happened to you?

Steven: Got cut, I guess.

Mom: What else?

Steven: I might have fallen down, but I didn't—I was real careful.

Mom: I'm glad you were careful, but the vase did get broken. And it was still the wrong thing to do, wasn't it?

Steven: Yes.

Mom: What should you think about next time?

Steven: It's wrong to take my toy without asking, and that I might get hurt if I climb on the furniture.

Mom: That's good thinking, Steven.

Steven: Can I have my toy now?

Mom: No. You'll have to give your toy back to me, and I'll keep it until Wednesday.

You Try It!

Rethinking is talking about your child's thinking after he has tested his skills. It can follow a good or bad, planned or unplanned event. By rethinking you can evaluate how well or poorly he formed opinions or made decisions. You can use it to decide if your child should be rewarded for good thinking or if correction is needed.

Jesus used rethinking to teach others how to think more like himself. Two good examples are recorded in Luke. You might like to read how he did it (Luke 10:1-23, especially verse 20, and Luke 7:36-50). Jesus certainly knew how to think about thinking!

Now prepare yourself to do a rethinking with your child. First read again the section called "Getting Ready to Rethink" in this chapter.

Gather the facts. What did your child do or say?

_____

_____

_____

_____

With your child, sort out what was wise thinking and what was foolish thinking.

wise thinking	foolish thinking
_____	_____
_____	_____
_____	_____
_____	_____
_____	_____

Ask your child to tell you what he or she is going to do the same next time as this time. What is going to be done differently?

do the same	do differently
_____	_____
_____	_____
_____	_____
_____	_____
_____	_____

How do you feel the rethinking went? What would you, as the rethinker, do differently next time?

———————————————————

———————————————————

———————————————————

———————————————————

CHAPTER TWELVE

Bible Search
and Research

The screen door banged as nine-year-old Brian ran inside the house. "Dad, look what I found in the back yard!" he yelled. In his cupped hands the catch of the day tried to escape to freedom. It was a huge, bright-green grasshopper.

Brian and his dad examined the strange creature. It had bulging, beady eyes and powerful hind legs. The wings on its back were longer than its body. As it hopped across their living room floor, Brian asked questions about his find. He wanted to know what it ate, how long it would live, how grasshoppers had babies, what they saw through their round eyes, and how God uses them. Dad realized he wasn't sure of any of the answers to Brian's questions. He suggested they do some research together. Brian agreed.

Helping your child to do research can be an exciting family activity. When he comes to you with questions about a discovery like Brian's, use his interest to teach research skills. By helping him learn to answer his own questions, you will teach him how to gather outside information. Teach him how to do a Bible search, how to research at home, and how to research at the public library. New gathering skills can then be put to use whenever he asks questions throughout his life. He will know how to find the answers he seeks. A childhood interest investigated can be the path to learning a life-long skill.

THE SEARCH IS ON

Choose a Subject

The first step in research is choosing a subject. Most children have plenty of interests. It isn't hard to find an idea to capture their fancy. If your child comes to you like Brian did with questions about some subject, follow up on that subject. Or take another approach—ask him some questions. Would he like to know more about a certain sport? Is he intrigued by ballet? Is there a kind of music he favors? What kinds of animals catch his eye? His answers to these questions are good topics for investigation.

Brian chose grasshoppers to be the subject of his study. It was a good choice because if he had chosen to research all insects, the task would have been too overwhelming. Choosing just one insect kept Brian's study within reasonable limits. Help your child narrow down his interest area to a small idea he can research easily.

List Key Words

Once the subject is chosen, have your child list some key words which describe it. First, encourage him to search his "inside" knowledge for other words which relate to his subject. Next, have him look up his main word in the dictionary. Definitions sometimes give synonyms which are good key words to follow up. This didn't work for Brian. When he looked up "grasshopper" in his junior-high level dictionary, it simply described his bug and gave an illustration. It didn't help him list key words. Brian's dad then showed Brian how to look up grasshopper in the family's thesaurus. This is the list they found under "grasshopper": locust, acridian, cicada, cicala, dog-day cicada, hopper, hoppergrass, cricket, cricket on the hearth.

Brian looked up each of these words in his dictionary. Some of the words weren't listed, but he did find several. He learned that a locust is a larger grasshopper-type bug. A cicada looked like a large fly. Dog-day meant the late part of summer. A hopper was something that hopped, and a cricket was related to a grasshopper, but it also made a chirping noise. Brian was surprised there were so many other bugs that were like his little green grasshopper.

After your child lists his key words, it is time to research further.

SEARCH THE BIBLE

Brian's dad suggested that the next step was to look at the Bible. Brian laughed. He couldn't imagine the Bible would give him any information about a grasshopper from his own back yard. Now it was Dad's turn to chuckle. He knew better.

Searching the Bible for information is an important part of thinking about God. The Bible contains all kinds of information about people, animals, places, history, and ideas. But Brian was right in believing the Bible sometimes does not address a subject we are researching. Automobiles, telephones, and space travel are not mentioned in God's Word. But in its pages, we *can* find out about transportation, communication, and the arrangement of stars in the heavens. Two-thousand-year-old principles can be applied to modern-day ideas. So if your child is working on a subject that is too modern to be specifically mentioned, look for a similar idea, or try to find a principle which applies to his subject.

The Searcher's Tools

Researchers need tools to help them find information about their subject. The tools of a Bible search are Bible reference books. Brian's family had several of these books on their shelf.

Dad helped Brian take down a few of them from the bookshelf to use in their Bible search about grasshoppers. The books Brian's dad chose were:

A Bible translation for young readers
A study Bible (for parent or older child)
A Bible concordance
A topical Bible
A Bible dictionary

Other books that are helpful when doing searches are Bible atlases, Bible handbooks, and

Bible encyclopedias. Commentaries on individual books of the Bible are also useful. Noel and I have listed several excellent examples of Bible reference books at the end of this chapter. Consider purchasing some of them for your family bookshelf if you don't already have them.

Using the Tools

Brian's Bible lay open before him on the table. "I don't know where to find out about grasshoppers in my Bible," he said. His dad explained the concordance and topical Bible would help them find passages which mention their insect friend. But first, Brian needed to pull out his list of key words.

Brian's dad explained that concordances and topical Bibles are arranged in alphabetical order just like Brian's English dictionary. But instead of a definition under each word, the Bible tool lists verses where the word can be found. A concordance lists verses that contain the actual word. The topical Bible lists words too, but also tells how the word is used.

After looking at his list, Brian found "grasshopper," "locust," and "cricket" in each book. He wrote down many of the references.

Reading Bible Verses

Brian and his dad read most of the verses together. They discovered that God said it was okay to eat locusts, grasshoppers, and crickets. John the Baptist ate locusts. Brian thought that sounded yucky. Brian also learned some people were afraid of locusts. In fact, God used locusts to punish Pharaoh when he wouldn't let Moses and the

Israelites leave Egypt. God also punished Israel with locusts when they wouldn't obey him.

Reading in Context

Brian found he could not understand some of the verses. His dad told him to read the whole paragraph and not just the verse.

That helped some, but he still had trouble understanding the meaning of some of the verses. So he and his dad read several paragraphs before the verse and several paragraphs after the verse. Now things made more sense. Brian had learned to read his verse *in context*.

What comes before and after a verse is important for understanding its meaning. When Brian first read about God punishing Pharaoh with the plague of locusts, he didn't understand that it was only the eighth of *ten* different plagues. When he read a few chapters before and after, he discovered the plague of locusts was one in a long string of punishments.

Brian was also confused by the way people acted and lived in Bible times. He couldn't understand why people were afraid of locusts. Brian needed to understand the *cultural context* too. To make their study easier, Brian and his dad decided to focus on the plague of locusts in Exodus 10. Dad decided it was time to look at some of the notes in his study Bible, look at the maps in the back of their Bibles, and look up some words such as "plague" and "locust" in the Bible dictionary.

Armed with their new cultural knowledge, they imagined what it was like to live in Egypt during the time of the plagues. As Brian looked at a map of

Egypt, he pretended he saw locusts coming up the Nile valley, blown by the wind. He imagined them coming in such a great swarm that they covered all the ground in his neighborhood. He could almost hear the crunching sound as people walked inside and outside their homes. The Bible said the locusts ate everything that was green. Brian looked outside and tried to imagine no grass and no gardens. He wondered what it would be like if all the trees and bushes had no leaves. Now he could see why the people were afraid of locusts.

Brian gained more information than he had ever imagined from doing a Bible search. He looked at his little green grasshopper. It looked harmless, but now he wondered.

SEARCH THE LIBRARY

Brian wanted to know if people today are still afraid of grasshoppers and locusts. His dad suggested they go to the public library and look up some current information on his insect.

Using Encyclopedias

The encyclopedia shelf was Brian's first stop in the library. He'd used encyclopedias at school before. Subjects were arranged in alphabetical order just like the dictionary. He found "grasshopper" and read the two-page article. The article told about each part of the grasshopper's body. He discovered that grass-hoppers lay eggs, and have not just one but five eyes!

Brian also read the article on locusts. It had a picture of a locust swarm. The swarm was worse than he had imagined.

Using the Card Catalog

After reading the encyclopedia articles, Brian went to the card catalog. He'd seen his dad use it before. There were thousands of cards in the little drawers. Where would grasshoppers be? Dad explained the card catalog is arranged in alphabetical order, too.

His dad explained that each book in the library has three kinds of cards. One is an author card. On this card the author's last name is written first, followed by his first name. Brian's name would be listed as: "Vance, Brian." Brian looked to see if there was a card with his name on it in the catalog. He found a "Vance, Andrew." No "Vance, Brian." The second kind of card has the title of the book at the top, followed by the author's name. It is a title card. The third type of card is a subject card. The subject of the book is typed at the top of the card in all capital letters, followed by the author's name and the book title. Brian would be looking for subject cards since he didn't know the name of an author who wrote about insects or a title of a book about grasshoppers.

Brian looked under the subject, "GRASS-HOPPER." He found five books that had something about his insect in them. He copied down the call number from each card, and the librarian helped him find the books. Brian also looked up "LOCUSTS" and "INSECTS." The books on locusts were the same as the "GRASSHOPPER" books. The "INSECT" books were about all kinds of bugs. Brian decided to check out three of the books he found. One was just about grasshoppers, the other two were general books about insects.

Using Periodicals

Brian was ready to leave, but his dad mentioned they might be able find some magazine articles on grasshoppers, too. Brain had never looked at the magazines in the library before. He was surprised when his dad said the library kept boxes of old magazines in a storage room. They could be checked out just like books.

Brian's dad led him to a table with a set of thick green books lined up in a row. The books were the *Reader's Guide to Periodical Literature.* Each book listed subjects in alphabetical order, and under each subject word were magazine articles which had been published that year on that subject.

Brian and his dad looked up "grasshoppers" in the *Reader's Guide.* They found two articles listed from magazines their library had in storage. They asked the librarian to find those magazines. One article was about grasshoppers eating crops in the western United States in 1985. The hoppers ate grass, alfalfa, wheat, potatoes, beans, and beets. They caused all sorts of problems. Even modern-day insecticides couldn't totally control the grasshoppers. The other article reported a swarm of locusts moving across northern Africa in 1987. The locusts had hatched near the Red Sea. Brian remembered reading about the locust plague in Egypt in Exodus 10. He decided present-day events really aren't so different from biblical events after all.

When Brian left the library, he had books to read at home. Now that he understood more about his grasshopper, he was interested in learning about other insects in his back yard. His dad had shown him how to research, and Brian was ready to get started on another subject.

Your child too can learn to research like Brian. Following this step-by-step method, he can begin to gather "outside" information at home, at the library, and from his Bible.

RECOMMENDED BOOKS FOR YOUR BIBLE SEARCH LIBRARY

The following books will help your family do Bible searches. Some of these are books written specifically for children. They are easy to read, but contain less information. Others are written for more accomplished readers. You may want to purchase them for yourself and for when your child is high school to college age. They contain more complete information.

Study Bibles: *Ryrie Study Bible, NIV Study Bible, The Adventure Bible*

Concordances: *NIV Complete Concordance, Young's Concordance*

Bible Dictionaries: *International Children's Bible Dictionary, NIV Compact Dictionary of the Bible, New Bible Dictionary*

Bible Handbooks: *International Children's Bible Handbook, Eerdman's Handbook to the Bible*

Topical Bible: *Nave's Compact Topical Bible, Nave's Topical Bible*

YOU TRY IT!

Help your child learn to answer his own questions. Bible Search and Research Skills will teach

him how to gather outside information. He will learn
how to do a Bible search, and how to gather
information outside the Bible.

What is the subject of your search?

_____

_____

_____

List the key words of your search. Look in the
sentence you just wrote, look in a dictionary, and
look in a thesaurus.

_____

_____

_____

_____

_____

Search the Bible. What did you find out about
your subject? Write your findings here.

_____

_____

_____

_____

_____

_____

Search the library. What did you find out about
your subject? Write your findings here.

_____

_____

_____

_____

_____

_____

The search is over. Write down the main things you have learned from your search, both from the Bible and from the library.

_____

_____

_____

_____

_____

_____

CHAPTER THIRTEEN

Media
Critique

Sarah and Josh were delighted to see an article in our local newspaper about their grade school principal, Pastor Rick. Pastor Rick and his wife love children. So much so that after numerous adoptions, they are now the parents of nineteen kids. It was great to see media attention paid to this wonderful family.

I had two reasons for wanting Sarah and Josh to read the article carefully. First, it would be fun to read about someone they knew. But second, the story contained an obvious mistake. I hoped my kids would discover it. Sarah saw it first. "Pastor Rick's wife isn't Betsy!" she cried. "Everybody knows her name is Jan."

"That's right," I said. "Did you know that newspaper writers sometimes make mistakes?" This was a great opportunity to teach my children some simple principles about learning from media.

WISDOM THINKING MEETS THE MEDIA

As Freddy the Fly buzzes through a typical American home, he sees media in every room he visits. Freddy walks across the newspaper spread out on the coffee table in the living room. Looking for someone to bother down the hall, he is blasted out of a teenager's room by a boom box transmitting weird noises. Fleeing to the den, Freddy ambles across the face of Dan Rather on the television screen. After being swatted away by an angry viewer, poor Freddy finally finds refuge in the bathroom. There he takes a nap on the latest issue of *Reader's Digest.*

As Freddy discovered, media is everywhere. And like Freddy, our kids usually don't have to go far to find information. Facts and ideas are available with a press of a button or a turn of a page. Communication networks bring the world to our doorstep. We can see the news happening on the other side of the world the moment it occurs. All thanks to modern media.

As helpful as media is, our children must also learn that the information gleaned from it cannot be used without caution. Someone else has done the gathering, sorting, and choosing with the facts and ideas. That person formed his own conclusion before passing it on to us. He may be a wise thinker, or he may not. Yet we make choices based on the information this other thinker provides. Teaching our children how to learn from print, film, and music is an important part of Wisdom Thinking training.

Learning the value and limitations of media will help your child make better use of the facts and ideas he gleans from these sources. So let's look at the three main types of media and discover how a Wisdom Thinker thinks about them.

News You Can Use

Sunday, May 18, 1980. John, Sarah, and I were returning from church. John switched on the car radio just as a song ended. The DJ broke the calm, and excitement, fear, and wonder echoed in his voice. "For those of you who haven't heard already," he said, "Mount St. Helens erupted at 8:32 this morning."

Hear It First on KNOW

Though we lived only fifty miles from Mount St. Helens, we hadn't heard the explosion that morning. Radio brought us the first report, and typical of a radio broadcast, after that brief update the music played on. Frustrated, I turned the dial to a station dedicated to news and talk shows. Callers were reporting what they could see of the ash plume from their homes, but their perceptions of what was going on at that moment varied widely.

Thirty seconds of news. The purpose of most radio stations is entertainment. Some news-only radio stations exist, but most stations, like the first one we listened to that morning, devote only a small portion of their air-time to current events. Stories must be important or entertaining to travel their airwaves.

If a teen's only source of news is from a typical radio station, her perspective of the world will be slightly skewed. We need to help our children fill out what they hear on the radio with a broader-based news source such as a newspaper or news magazine. The radio condenses complex issues and events into short spots. The information is current, but it isn't complete.

Who's talking? Talk shows are popular on radio. We can hear anyone from former presidents to the neighbor next door talking about subjects as varied as UFOs and nuclear waste. But it's hard to evaluate sources on the radio. When St. Helens erupted, one caller made it sound like Seattle had been blown off the face of the earth. Ideas can be gleaned from these shows, but they must be investigated further and researched carefully.

John and I weren't satisfied with the small snatch of news we gathered from the car radio that morning. Along with everyone else in the Pacific Northwest, we had watched the mountain awaken, and we wanted to know as much as possible about what was going on. So when we got home, the first thing we did was turn on the TV.

See It to Believe It

Every major television station in Portland was covering the eruption. We flipped from channel to channel to hear interviews with geologists and eyewitnesses. The pictures of the ash plume were overwhelming. The radio had not at all conveyed to us the massive nature of this latest eruption, but television did.

TV is a spectator sport. Television is a *visual* medium. The point of having a TV in your living room is to be able to watch what happened. When stories are chosen for broadcast, those with the greatest visual impact are most likely to be shown. That's why we see the rare volcano eruptions but not the common sleeping mountains. We see the plane crashes but not the successful take-offs and landings. Again, as with newspapers, this limits our opportunity to gather *all* the facts. Not all mountains explode like Mount St. Helens. Not all planes crash. But if it doesn't catch your eye, you won't often see it on TV.

TV news is also entertainment. Television is also an *entertainment* medium. Facts mix with fluff. During the St. Helens reports, news editors limited the number of interviews with geological experts. Instead we heard from press liaisons who make the news more interesting to all viewers. Eyewitnesses gave their biased accounts. Television takes this approach because serious debates by experts and authorities do not hold the audience's attention. Phil Donahue bouncing through the audience eliciting opinions is more fun. But is this factual information? Maybe. But mostly, it's entertainment.

As with radio, television reports some of the facts, but not all. It is a good source for ideas, but we must teach our children to gather from other sources for a complete picture of an event or issue.

Read All about It

Monday morning, May 19th, we read all about the eruption in the *Oregonian* newspaper. There were pictures, maps, first-person accounts, and analyses. Through the newspaper reports, we could begin to put the facts together in a more understandable way.

Later, the weekly news magazines such as *Time, Newsweek*, and *U.S. News & World Report* covered the eruption in greater depth. Reporters from these periodicals had a longer time to sift through and separate facts from fiction. Their stories were brief, but they offered a distilled and clearer picture of the events of May 18th.

Finally, months later, books on the eruption of Mount St. Helens hit the stores. The books were visual. The authors were able to choose the best of the photos for publication. The books were informational. They told the story in an organized and understandable way. And the books were accurate. The authors had plenty of time to gather, sort, and choose before they wrote their stories.

When teaching our children to use newspapers, magazines, and books for information, we need to help them think about these things:

Who is giving out this information? Some books, magazines, and newspaper are not worth the paper they are printed on. No doubt some supermarket tabloid attributed the eruption of St. Helens to Bigfoot falling into the crater. We need to help our kids see the worthlessness of these types of publications.

In addition, editors, newspapers, and writers declare political and social stands. We can find out what political party or social causes our paper supports by reading the editorial page. That bias will affect what stories are covered, how they are reported, and what facts are included. If we're aware of this bias, we can help our children learn to identify it.

When our kids read books, we need to teach them to learn about the writer. Sometimes we can find out about that person's personal views. Is he involved in the New Age movement, Scientology, or some other cult? Maybe he's an atheist. It makes a difference if he's politically liberal or conservative. If the author has an axe to grind, his work will reflect that bias.

Are these all the facts? It's not possible to get all the facts all the time. Radio broke the news on Mount St. Helens, television gave the visual story, newspapers and magazines drew a larger picture, and books gave the most in-depth study. Yet all media are limited by the reporter or writer's gathering, sorting, and choosing.

Radio, TV, and newspapers are limited by time; newspapers and magazines are limited by space. All have deadlines to meet so fact-gathering time is short. Sometimes important information is left out. "Normal" life is rarely reported because it isn't "news." Exceptions to normal life are given the most press. This imbalance can lead to faulty perceptions about what is happening in the world. The bias of the writer or editor may influence how facts are presented, what is said, and what isn't.

Do I see the big picture? Radio, television, newspapers, magazines, and books each give information in their own way. Gathering from all kinds of sources to gain an over-all perspective of an event or issue can provide a bigger picture. Radio, TV, and newspapers keep us current, magazines add details, books give us greater depth.

BUY IT, YOU'LL LIKE IT

Once when Josh and I went shopping a couple of years ago, he got all excited when he spotted a box of *Oxy 10* on the store shelf. Josh said, "*Oxy 10* is better than *Stridex*. If you use *Stridex* a big box will fall out of the sky and land on your head." Fortunately, I'd seen the commercial which was the source of Josh's nugget of wisdom. If I hadn't, I would have been concerned about his sanity. As it was, this incident underscored the great influence advertising has on kids and adults. Josh had seen a box fall on a kid who used *Stridex,* and until we talked it over in the store, he believed it might happen to him if he used the wrong product.

Evaluating advertising is a good exercise for Wisdom Thinkers. Advertisements appear in print, on television, and on the radio. You'll find them on billboards and painted on signs on your neighbor's lawn. Advertising is such a part of American life that it's easy to forget it's purpose.

The goal of advertising is to sell a product. Advertisements sell things, ideas, events, or people. Advertising tries to get something from you. Sometimes it tries to get your vote. Usually it tries to get your money. It's that simple.

But teaching kids to walk away from the advertiser's gimmicks isn't simple. Advertisers manipulate their audience in many ways. Every child needs to know how to untangle himself from the advertiser's web. The following concepts will help you teach your child to think wisely about what he sees, reads, and hears:

You'll feel good if you buy . . . Ads aimed at kids often focus on feelings. Make-up for preteens makes little girls *feel* grown up. GI Joe equipment makes boys *feel* like men. Rock stars have their own 800 numbers where callers can hear a recorded message taped by the star. Callers have a slim chance to *feel* special because the star actually answers in person now and then. But these ads sell *fleeting feelings.* They offer happiness that is only temporal. But the agencies who devise these ads know people want to feel good at almost any cost. They know if their product offers to makes us feel good, we are more likely to buy it.

You'll look just like them if you buy . . . The tobacco industry shows only healthy, good-looking smokers. None of them cough, none go to the doctor for cancer treatment. All the smokers look beautiful. And we will too, they imply, if we smoke or chew.

Beautiful models advertise make-up, shampoo, face cream, and clothes hinting we can be stunning if we buy those products. But no one mentions that true beauty is more than skin deep.

You'll feel left out unless you buy . . . Many children are shown playing with the "toy you've just got to have." "Tommy, Julie, Katie, and Peter have one. You should have one too!" A child watching the ad feels he's the only kid in the world without that toy. If only Mom would buy him that toy, he would be like all the other kids.

You'll be right if you buy . . . Mrs. Average American is asked to decide which of two peanut butters tastes best. She chooses jar number one. The narrator whips the cover off the label and proudly announces another confirmation that his peanut butter is best of all. There's only one catch. Mrs. A. American had no chance to taste all the other peanut butter brands on the market.

These tactics and others are used by advertisers to prey on our kids. The advertising industry uses their innocence to pressure them into buying products. What can you do? Most children are greatly helped by having an adult explain the difference between programs and commercials. Sometimes they don't know the difference. When our kids are older, we can explain the tactics outlined above. Once they know that advertising tries to make them buy something, they are less influenced by its claims.

THAT'S ENTERTAINMENT?

School's out for the day. Dad and Mom are home from work. Dinner's over, the table's been cleared, the dishwasher is running. Let's kick off our shoes, sit down, and relax. It's been a long day, and it's time for some entertainment. What shall it be? A book? A TV show? A movie on the VCR? Or maybe some music. Whatever we choose, and whatever our children choose, we'd better stop and think about it. Because entertainment is a media form that needs our Wisdom Thinking.

Fiction Books

Mom's so proud. Charlie's a reader—he would rather read than watch TV! That makes her happy. Books are so much better than those mindless sitcoms. And as long as he's safely in his room, she knows he's all right. But is he?

Teaching kids to think about the fiction they read is extremely important. Mindless sitcoms pale in comparison to the mental images some modern fiction can conjure up. In addition to being aware of the books our kids read, we need to teach them to ask two simple questions about the content of the stories they enjoy:

How do the characters think and make choices? Do the characters think before they act? What happens when they don't? Which characters do I admire most? Why do I admire them? What do the characters do that please God? What do the characters do that does not please God?

Is this story helpful to me? Did I enjoy this book? Why? Does this book help me think more wisely about others? Did I learn anything I can apply to my own life? What ideas are not helpful?

Television and Movies

Bill and Connie Parker are raising their children without a television in their home. They don't miss it, and their kids, still grade-school age, barely remember the days of Saturday morning cartoons. The Parkers do take in a movie now and then. Usually it's a Walt Disney cartoon they all enjoy.

Ron and Carol Bishop have a TV. They watch programs almost every evening, but the kids must finish their homework first. They go to movies, too, more regularly than the Parkers. And they see a variety of films that Ron and Carol preview before taking their children.

Which couple is "raising their kids right"? They both could be. Whichever family seems most like yours, here are some guidelines to help your child learn to be a wise viewer:

The TV has an off switch and the theater has an exit. Control the media. Don't let it control your life. John and I went to a movie many years ago and sat near a couple we knew from church. The movie began. It wasn't particularly offensive to us, but the other couple got up and left after the first twenty minutes. I've always remembered their action. Turning a program off or leaving the theater is the ultimate critical statement. Make that statement when you feel it is necessary.

Think as you watch. We need to watch and discuss movies and programs with our kids. It's helpful to talk with them about what we liked and what we didn't like about the show. When our kids are teens, if a program we're watching contains slightly objectionable material, it could be best to leave it on and discuss it together. Switching channels abruptly sometimes makes the program more enticing. Discussing what's good and bad may diffuse the program's appeal.

Remember the power of television and movies to manipulate. The music played during movies and TV shows is designed to raise certain emotions in the audience. Take the music away and the power of a scene is gone. After only a few months of television watching, children are programmed to respond emotionally. Laugh tracks accomplish the same feat. We become programmed to laugh when the director says it's time to laugh. What shouldn't be funny, becomes funny. And that's no laughing matter!

Music

Young Wisdom Thinkers need to learn to evaluate music. Music, inside and outside the church, is a powerful influence. Rhythm and beat make words memorable. That can be good, or it can be bad.

We can control what our children hear at home, but music is played almost everywhere young people like to be. In these days of portable entertainment, if our child doesn't bring the music, someone else's child certainly will. The following suggestions will help you teach your child to think about what she hears:

How does this music make me feel? Music has power to soothe the savage beast. But it can also bring out the beast! Just as a musical score in a TV program or movie manipulates feelings, so do songs alone. We need to encourage our kids to think about how different types of music, secular and Christian, make them feel. Uplifted or angry? Calm or unsettled? Happy or sad?

What do the words say? What attitudes does the songwriter express? Do our children agree with his attitudes? Are they consistent with Bible teaching? Does the song focus on ideas Christians want to think about? When our kids wake up in the morning is this song the one they want running through their heads?

Who wrote the song and who sings it? Does our child want to look and behave like the people who sing these songs? What is admirable about them? What is not? Does our child want to support these people financially by buying their music?

Is this music helping me to be a better Wisdom Thinker? When this music is played, how does it affect thinking? Does it confuse thinking like strong emotion? Or is it a positive addition to her inside information? Do the words encourage her to act without thinking? Or does the song add new perspective which will help her make better choices?

Media can be helpful if used wisely. You can teach your child to use it like a Wisdom Thinker by doing the following activities:

YOU TRY IT!

News

Reporters and journalists bring us the facts. They give us the information in three ways: they write it in books, newspapers, and magazines, they tell it over the radio, and they show it to us on television.

What are the facts of the news story?

_____

_____

_____

_____

What is the source of the news story?

_____

_____

_____

_____

What facts might be missing from the story?

_____

_____

_____

_____

Where can you go to find other information about this news story?

_____

_____

_____

_____

What's the big picture of the news story?

_____

_____

_____

_____

Advertising

The goal of advertising is to sell a product. Advertisements appear in print, on television, and on the radio. Advertisements sell things, ideas, events, or people. Advertising tries to get something from you. Sometimes it tries to get your vote; usually it tries to get your money. It's that simple.

What is being sold?

_____

_____

_____

Why are you being told you should buy this particular product?

_____

_____

_____

Name the other brands of this same product.

_____

_____

_____

_____

_____

Is this brand better than the similar brands? How do you know it's better?

_____

_____

_____

_____

Do you have to buy now?

yes_____ no_____

Entertainment

Entertainment fills many hours of a child's life and comes in many forms. A book lets a child's imagination fly. Television, movies, and videos fill their minds with millions of pictures of the world around them. And music comforts, energizes, or makes them smile. Each has its value, each has its drawbacks, all entertain.

List below the title of the movie, song, TV program, or book you want to critique.

_____

Gather "inside" and "outside" information about the title.

inside information   outside information

_____   _____

_____   _____

_____   _____

_____   _____

_____   _____

Sort the "inside" and "outside" information you collected into what's good about the entertainment, what's bad about the entertainment, and what's questionable about the entertainment.

good   questionable   bad

_____   _____   _____

_____   _____   _____

_____   _____   _____

—————————————

———————   ———————   ———————

———————   ———————   ———————

Choose to be entertained by this title, or choose to look elsewhere for entertainment. What did you choose?

—————————————

Putting It All Together

Craig (8) and his little sister Kendall (6) had trouble sharing. At least six times a day, the house rang with their shouts: "That's mine! Give it back to me!" Mom was near the end of her rope. She had tried reasoning with them, but it seemed that Craig and Kendall weren't willing to change their ways.

So Mom decided to focus on thinking about sharing. She devised a mental plan of when they could do some special sharing activities. After looking through the methods in this section, she saw several she could use during the next couple of weeks. This is what she did:

Monday

Craig and Kendall came home from school. It was a rainy day and they had to stay inside. Both wanted to watch television, but Craig wanted to watch "Batman" and Kendall wanted to watch "Duck Tales." The fight began. Both kids were screaming in a matter of seconds.

Mom decided a Rethinking was in order. She turned off the TV and sat both kids down on the couch. First order of business was gathering the facts—who wanted to watch what and why? Craig told his side, Kendall told hers. Then Mom helped them sort through thinking. Since they did not have two TV sets, they would have to choose. That meant compromise. Mom asked if either of them had an idea of how they could choose what to do about their problem. Craig suggested they each pick one half-hour program each day. Kendall agreed. But who would choose first? Kendall said at school they drew straws. Mom thought that was a good way to be fair, so they each drew. Craig got to choose first.

Craig asked if he would get to choose first every day. Mom said no, next time it would be Kendall's turn. And she wrote it on the calendar so no one would forget.

Wednesday

Wednesday was the family's day to go to the library. Mom always checked out storybooks to read to the kids. This week, she decided to look for a story that emphasized sharing. She remembered a book from her childhood called *Mrs. Piggle-Wiggle.* It was a collection of stories about a wonderful woman who knew just how to cure children of bad habits.

She looked up the book in the card catalog and found it on the shelf. Sure enough, it had a "Selfishness Cure." Mom checked it out to read at home that evening.

Just before bed, Craig and Kendall settled down for their evening story. They learned all about a boy named Dick Thompson. He was selfish about everything. It was a funny story and they laughed at the great lengths Dick's parents went to cure Dick of his selfishness. But when the story was over, Kendall said, "Sometimes I'm like Dick and I don't want Craig to play with my toys." Kendall prayed that evening and asked God to help her become less selfish.

Friday

Friday evening Craig noticed his dad was reading his Bible. He asked what he was reading. Dad explained he was reading about David and Jonathan who were great friends. He told Craig how Jonathan was the son of Saul who was king of Israel. Dad explained the custom of sons becoming king when their father died. He said, "If I were king of our country, when I died, you would become king." Craig thought about how neat that would be. He said, "Would I be rich and get to tell people what to do?" Dad said, "Yes." Then he asked Craig, "Do you think you would like to be a king?" Craig nodded.

Craig asked, "When Saul died, did Jonathan become king?" Dad said, "No. God chose David to be king instead." Craig cried, "That isn't fair! Wasn't Jonathan angry? I bet he wanted to kill David!" Dad said, "You might expect him to be angry, but Jonathan was very unselfish. He loved David, and he knew God had chosen David to be the next king. Jonathan was willing to be second to David."

Craig was amazed by Jonathan's behavior. He said, "I bet David was happy to have a friend like Jonathan." Dad agreed and said, "An unselfish friend is the best kind of friend."

Saturday

Saturday morning, Mom awoke to the sound of Saturday morning cartoons. She went out to see what the kids were watching. They had agreed on a show together without fighting. Mom was pleased.

She sat down to watch the "Smurfs" with the kids. One point brought up in the program was the selfishness of one of the characters. Mom said, "I'm glad that Smurf doesn't live in my home." Craig said, "He needs Mrs. Piggle-Wiggle's Selfishness Cure."

Later in the day, as Mom looked back over the week, she was happy about the emphasis she and her husband had placed on thinking about unselfish behavior. The kids were still fighting some over what was theirs. But now and then they laughed about needing Mrs. Piggle-Wiggle's "Selfishness Cure." It showed Mom that they were thinking more wisely about their behavior. And that was the whole point.

A Final Word

Wisdom Thinking is a way of life. Gathering, Sorting, and Choosing; Thinking about Thinking; Thinking about God. These three skills are like a weaver's strands woven through each idea and every choice. They should be part of all thoughts, whether large or small.

Teaching our children to weave Wisdom Thinking into their lives prepares them for all sorts of decisions. During their lifetimes they will have millions of opportunities to use the thinking skills they have learned. And they will need these skills to guide their thinking and choice-making.

But sometimes it's difficult for us to be patient while our children develop and grow. As diligent as we may be, this truth remains: Wisdom does not develop overnight. And even skilled use of Wisdom Thinking does not guarantee totally wise choices every time. But time is a great teacher, and maturity and experience will continue to add needed perspective to our children's store of knowledge. We may not see changes overnight, but they are taking place.

Remember, it's worth the wait. And while we're waiting, we'll know we've done much to help our children learn to live wisely. For we will have fulfilled our responsibility to prepare our children for life. We will have given our children the skills they need to make wise choices. When the day comes for our children to make wise choices, they will be able to because we will have taught them how.

So as we're teaching, watching, and waiting, let's also pray. We need God's wisdom for our children and ourselves. Let's pray for the present, that God will help us communicate what our kids need to know and that he will help our children understand. And let's pray for the future. Let's pray continually that the Lord will enable our children to remember how to think with wisdom as they face difficult decisions in our world of countless choices.

A Selected
Bibliography

Adams, James L. *Conceptual Blockbusting: A Guide to Better Ideas*. Menlo Park, Calif.: Addison-Wesley Publishing, 1986.

Adler, Mortimer. " 'Critical Thinking' Programs: Why They Won't Work." *The Education Digest,* March 1987, 9-11.

_____. *How to Read a Book*. New York: Simon and Schuster, 1972.

Bauer, Gary. "Teaching Morality in the Classroom." *The Education Digest,* March 1987, 2-5.

Bergmann, Sherrel. "Teaching Middle-Schoolers Decision-Making Skills." *The Education Digest,* March 1987, 48-50.

Bowen, Ezra. "Can Colleges Teach Thinking?" *Time,* 16 February 1987, 61.

Chance, Paul. "Master of Mastery." *Psychology Today,* April 1987, 43-46.

Chance, Paul and Joshua Fischman. "The Magic of Childhood." *Psychology Today,* May 1987, 48-59.

Cleveland, Harlan. "Educating Citizens and Leaders for an Information-Based Society." *The Education Digest,* September 1986, 2-5.

Costa, Arthur L. "Teaching for Intelligent Behavior." Sacramento: California State University, 1988. Mimeo.

de Bono, Edward. "A Technique for Teaching Creative Thinking." *Momentum,* September 1986, 17-19.

_____. "Clear Thinking May Depend on the 'Hat' You Wear; Interview with Edward de Bono." *U.S. News & World Report,* 2 December 1985, 75-76.

_____. *de Bono's Thinking Course.* New York: Facts on File, 1985.

Dunkley, Christopher. "TV's Distorted Window on the World." *World Press Review,* April 1987, 64.

Dworkin, Peter. "The Value of 'Values Education.' " *U.S. News & World Report,* 23 February 1987, 61.

Ennis, Robert H. "A Logical Basis for Measuring Critical Thinking Skills." *Educational Leadership,* October 1985, 44-48.

_____. "Critical Thinking and the Curriculum." *National Forum,* Winter 1985, 28-31.

Fee, Gordon D. and Douglas Stuart. *How to Read the Bible for All It's Worth: A Guide to Understanding the Bible.* Grand Rapids, Mich.: Zondervan Publishing House, 1982.

Garofalo, Joe. "Developing Metacognition for School Mathematics." *The Education Digest,* December 1987, 48-50.

Glaser, Edward M. "Critical Thinking: Educating for Responsible Citizenship in a Democracy." *National Forum,* Winter 1985, 24-29.

Halpern, Diane. *Thought & Knowledge.* Hillsdale, N.J.: Lawrence Erlbaum Assoc., 1984.

Henniger, Michael L. "Learning Mathematics and Science Through Play." *Journal of Research in Childhood Education* (February 1987):167-71.

Hunt, Gladys. *Honey for a Child's Heart.* Grand Rapids, Mich.: Zondervan Publishing House, 1978.

Kealey, Robert J. "The Present Task: Thinking and Valuing Skills." *Momentum,* September 1986, 14-16.

Kobrin, Beverly. *Eyeopeners! How to Choose and Use Children's Books About Real People, Places, and Things.* New York: Viking Penguin, 1988.

Kohn, Alfie. "How to Succeed Without Even Vying." *Psychology Today,* September 1986, 22-28.

Lichter, S. Robert, Stanley Rothman, and Linda S. Lichter. *The Media Elite.* Bethesda, Md.: Adler & Adler, 1986.

Lindskoog, John and Kathryn Lindskoog. *How to Grow a Young Reader.* Wheaton, Ill.: Harold Shaw Publishers, 1989.

Lipman, Matthew. "Philosophy for Children and Critical Thinking." *National Forum*, Winter 1985, 18-23.

Lippert, Barbara. "Lying With a Smile on Madison Avenue." *U.S. News & World Report*, 23 February 1987, 58.

Lockwood, Alan L. "Public Secondary Schools and Moral Education." *The Education Digest*, October 1988, 15-18.

Marbach, William D. and Connie Leslie. "Why Johnny Can't Reason." *Newsweek*, 27 January 1986, 59.

Martia, Dominic. "Putting Reading in its Proper Place." *U.S. News & World Report*, 9 February 1987, 6.

Nehmer, Nancy L. *A Parent's Guide to Christian Books for Children*. Wheaton, Ill.: Tyndale House Publishers, 1984.

Newmann, Fred M. "Higher-Order Thinking in High School." *The Education Digest*, December 1988, 23-27.

Nickerson, Raymond S. "On Improving Thinking Through Instruction." In vol. 15 of *Review of Research in Education*, edited by Ernst Z. Rothkopf, 3-57. Washington, D.C.: American Educational Research Association, 1988.

Paul, Richard W. "The Critical-Thinking Movement: A Historical Perspective." *National Forum*, Winter 1985, 2.

Postman, Neil. *Amusing Ourselves to Death*. New York: Penguin Books, 1985.

_____. "Critical Thinking in the Electronic Era." *National Forum,* Winter 1985, 4.

Power, Clark and Lawrence Kohlberg. "Using a Hidden Curriculum for Moral Education." *The Education Digest,* May 1987, 10-13.

Rothman, Stanley and Robert Lerner. "Television and the Communications Revolution." *Society,* November/December 1988, 64-70.

Sabini, John and Maury Silver. "Critical Thinking and Obedience to Authority." *National Forum,* Winter 1985, 13-17.

Saterlie, Mary Ellen. "A Community-Based Values Program." *The Education Digest,* December 1988, 34-37.

Sattes, Beth. "Parental Involvement in Student Learning." *The Education Digest,* January 1989, 37-39.

Scriven, Michael. "Critical for Survival." *National Forum,* Winter 1985, 9-12.

Slife, Brant D. and Ruth E. Cook. "Developing Problem-Solving Skills." *The Education Digest,* February 1986, 50-53.

Trelease, Jim. *The Read-Aloud Handbook.* New York: Viking Penguin, 1985.

Wynne, Edward A. "Transmitting Moral Values." *The Education Digest,* April 1986, 26-29.